Messing With Tourists

Stupid Answers To Stupid Questions

Best Wishes and Enjoy the Toilet Book!

Alex Stokes 2014

Alex Stokes

Copyright © 2013 Alex Stokes

All rights reserved.

ISBN:1483974863
ISBN-13:9781483974866

DEDICATION

I would like to dedicate this book first and foremost to my beautiful wife Jenny, who has supported me and driven me to write my crazy thoughts on paper. Also, to all of my family, who have supported me through the rough times in order to pursue my dream of Comedy. To my children, who think I'm crazy and not funny most of the time, but who love me nonetheless. To my friends and fans, who have kept me in the Comedy world this long. To Gary Woods Photography, who did a wonderful job designing and shooting the cover. Last, but certainly not least, to the crazy tourists who made this all possible with their idiotic questions.

CONTENTS

i

Chapter 1: Stupidity

Ok, who am I kidding. The whole thing is stupid.

PREFACE

. This book is a collection of conversations I had while sitting in a booth in Gatlinburg, TN. One of the largest tourist destinations in America, Gatlinburg has millions of visitors every year who come to enjoy the Mountains, Attractions, T-Shirt shops and Pancakes. During this time in the booth, I was asked some of the craziest, most insane questions a human could ask. So, after several hundred of these, I decided it was time to answer them back in my own special way. It is important to note that even the normal questions, if asked rudely, were given my own special response. Please note: Normal Tourists were not harmed during the making of this book.

If life hands you lemons, then there is a very small chance that your grocery store bagger's name was Life.

~Alex Stokes~

#1 ARE DOGS ALLOWED?

Me: Nice dog!
Tourist: Thank you! Hey, could you tell us if dogs are allowed in the mountains?
Me: I doubt it. They don't like animals running around in the woods.
Tourist: That's strange.
Me: I know.
Tourist: I can't even walk my dog on the trails?
Me: You could I guess. I just wouldn't recommend it.
Tourist: Why is that?
Me: They are having a problem with squirrels with red eyes attacking dogs.
Tourist: Seriously?
Me: Yep. It's the craziest thing I've ever heard.
Tourist: Why do they have red eyes?
Me: Well, apparently some people's camera lenses are messed up.
Tourist: Oh…ha, ha, ha. So they don't really have red eyes?
Me: I dunno. I've seen pictures and they are definitely red.
Tourist: So how many dogs have been attacked?
Me: I'd say there have been 15 Rabid Red Eyed Squirrel attacks in the last year.
Tourist: That many have been reported?
Me: Oh. No, I've never heard of one being reported. Just my estimation.
Tourist: How are you estimating that if none have been reported? Based on what exactly?
Me: The Laws of Gravity.
Tourist: Huh?
Me: The Laws of Physics. I usually say Gravity first. It's a problem I have.
Tourist: Neither of those make any sense.
Me: Oh, I know. I usually follow those up with another theory.
Tourist: And what would that be?
Me: The Laws of Attraction.
Tourist: Oh Geez.
Me: I know. They are all wrong. But I'm not really a lawyer you know.
Tourist: You are definitely one of the oddest people we've met since we've been here.
Me: Really? You guys think I'm odder than most of the other people you've met around here?
Tourist: Yes.
Me: Thank you. I honestly mean that.

#2 THE WATERFALL

Tourist: Hello! Do you know where to find the best waterfall in the mountains?
Me: Sure. First, define "Best." Then, Define "Waterfall." No need to define mountains though.
Tourist: Ooooo Kkkkkk....By best I mean tallest, and by waterfall I mean falling water off of rocks or something.
Me: That's what I figured.
Tourist: So do you know?
Me: Yes.
Tourist: And?
Me: Well, first you need to go into the mountains.
Tourist: I figured that much.
Me: So you already know it all then? Why are you asking me?
Tourist: No, that was just common sense.
Me: Fine. So, go into the mountains and take a left.
Tourist: Huh? Take a left? Take a left where???
Me: Between the trees. Two tall ones.
Tourist: You are making this extremely difficult.
Me: That's my job, Sir.
Tourist: Whatever. So, I take a left then what?
Me: I'm going to tell you.
Tourist: Ok. Then tell me.
Me: Go up a hill. There will be more trees. Like an excessive amount of trees.
Tourist: (angry) Ok.
Me: Listen for water.
Tourist: Ok.
Me: Look for a Ceramic Donkey.
Tourist: Ok, this is getting to be ridiculous.
Me: I know. I just love to say the word Donkey.
Tourist: Ok, please be serious or I'll ask someone else.
Me: Fine. I was just messing with you. Don't take a left. Take a right.
Tourist: Really?
Me: No. I'm not finished messing with you yet.
Tourist: Ok. Thanks so much for no help.
Me: That didn't even make any sense. But you are very welcome.

#3 DE'BEARS

Tourist: Hiiiiii....I have a really strange and probably stupid question.
Me: I'm sure my answer will match you.
Tourist: Huh?
Me: Never mind. Proceed.
Tourist: Ok. Well, uh, do you guys ever have a problem with bears breeding with deer? I know that's a strange question.
Me: (turning around for a second to gather myself) Well, I wouldn't necessarily call it a "problem."
Tourist: Ohhhh....so you guys have it happen then?
Me: Of course. There are several De'Bears running around.
Tourist: You ever see one?
Me: Once.
Tourist: What it look like?
Me: A bear with tiny antlers.
Tourist: Hmmm. Not what I thought it would look like.
Me: I honestly can't believe you've actually pictured one in your head before.
Tourist: I think about it every time we visit. You are the first person to not think I'm crazy.
Me: No. You're crazy.
Tourist: Huh?
Me: I made it up. I've never, ever seen one.
Tourist: Seriously? That's not a nice prank.
Me: Seriously dude...a bear with tiny antlers? You deserved it.
Tourist: You know it has to happen sometimes. That's nature.
Me: Ok please stop. I really can't take it. Am I on hidden camera?
Tourist: No, I'm being dead serious. It has had to happen sometime before.
Me: No, it hasn't had to happen.
Tourist: You honestly don't think a bear and deer have ever gotten together before, in the history of the world?
Me: Well, we are in Tennessee. You may be right.
Tourist: I know I'm right.
Me: Okee Dokee.
Tourist: So, you at least believe it's a possibility now?
Me: No. You are still nuts.

#4 THE DEER STAND

Tourist: Excuse me man, is there a good place to rent a tree stand up here for hunting?
Me: What are you hunting?
Tourist: Deer.
Me: Oh. Well, I don't know about tree stands, but the top of that building would be cheaper.
Tourist: That building?
Me: Yup. See it? It's really high. You could probably do well up there if you have binoculars.
Tourist: Are you crazy man?
Me: A little bit, yes.
Tourist: Man, I'm pretty sure that's not legal.
Me: Well, I see it this way. It's one of those things where you just play stupid if you get caught. Like you had no idea it was illegal. I'm sure they would be very lenient.
Tourist: Seriously man, you are nuts.
Me: You are the one who is wanting to sit in a tree stand and shoot deer.
Tourist: Well that's how you do it.
Me: Why is that?
Tourist: Because it's easier to spot the deer and shoot them from there.
Me: So, you're saying you are not good at hunting?
Tourist: No I'm not!!!
Me: Not saying that or you are not good at hunting?
Tourist: (agitated) I'm not saying that!!!
Me: Oh. That's right. I said that.
Tourist: Let me ask you man…do you hunt?
Me: Of course.
Tourist: What do you hunt?
Me: All kinds of stuff. Depends though.
Tourist: On what? The Season?
Me: No. It depends on what the little guide on my video game says is in the woods around my hunter on the screen.

THE DEER STAND CONTINUED……

Tourist: Hahaha. So, you don't even hunt? You just sit on your couch shooting video game animals and you have the nerve to tell me I'm not a good hunter?
Me: No, I never said I sit on my couch. I have a tree stand in the living room.
Tourist: Are you mocking me?
Me: No. Yes.
Tourist: You better watch yourself.

#5 MOUNTAINS CLOSED

Tourist: Excuse me, I have a question.
Me: Ok good. I have an answer.
Tourist: Huh?
Me: Never mind. Go ahead.
Tourist: How late are the mountains open?
Me: Well, during the slow season, the animals usually close at 8. Except the bats, they work late.
Tourist: What are you talking about?
Me: The better question is what are you talking about?
Tourist: I meant what time is too late to go in the mountains?
Me: If you get eaten by a bear, then it's too late.
Tourist: Are you trying to be funny?
Me: Yes. I'm trying really hard.

#6 BACKROADS

Tourist: Hi there!!!
Me: YOLO.
Tourist: Huh?
Me: Sorry. I've always wanted to start a conversation by saying that.
Tourist: Oh. Haha. So, could you tell me where the best back road is around here?
Me: You just want to know the best general back road?
Tourist: Yes.
Me: Do you even know where you are going?
Tourist: Yes.
Me: Ok. That's all the information I think I need.
Tourist: Great!!
Me: So, start off by driving about 15 miles east.
Tourist: Ok.
Me: Take a left at the 13th road you come to. I'm sorry but I can't remember the name of the road.
Tourist: Oh, no problem. 13th road. I got it.
Me: Ok. Take the 3rd left on that road and go 15 miles west.
Tourist: Hmmm, Ok.
Me: That will possibly bring you back here.
Tourist: Well, that's not where I was wanting to go.
Me: It's by far the best back road though.
Tourist: Yeah, but I don't need to do that.
Me: Well you didn't tell me where you wanted to go.
Tourist: Oh…haha, sorry! We are trying to get home.
Me: Ohhh…why didn't you say that?
Tourist: Again. Sorry.
Me: No problem. Well, still take the 13th road, but stay straight for 30 miles instead of turning left.
Tourist: Where will that take me?
Me: To my home.
Tourist: No, I meant my home.
Me: Ummm, Sir, I have no idea where you live.
Tourist: Oh, did I forget to tell you that?
Me: Yes.
Tourist: Why didn't you ask me then?
Me: Because I was really enjoying our conversation, and I didn't want it to end. Like they say, YOLO.

#7 PETTING ZOO

Tourist: Hey...is there a petting zoo close?
Me: You want to pay or free?
Tourist: Well free of course!
Me: It's in the mountains.
Tourist: Off the side of the road?
Me: Yes. There are signs. They say "warning, bears have been seen here recently. Do not feed!" Just ignore the signs.
Tourist: (not catching on here) Why would a zoo put up a sign like that?
Me: Well, zoo is just the technical term.
Tourist: Technical for what?
Me: Wilderness.
Tourist: Ohhhhh....I get it. You are messing with me.
Me: No. You can pet the animals.
Tourist: Yeah, I'm not prepared to do that.
Me: Well, all you need is a hairbrush and hand sanitizer, or "hanitizer" as my son calls it. He's a funny little boy.
Tourist: Sounds like it.
Me: He is.
Tourist: So, there isn't a real petting Zoo around here?
Me: There is a fake one.
Tourist: Are you still messing with me?
Me: Kind of.
Tourist: Do you always do this?
Me: No. Only when people ask me stupid questions or if they are rude.
Tourist: Which was I then?
Me: I'd say both.
Tourist: This has been an interesting conversation.
Me: No, it really hasn't.

#8 THE NEWLYWEDS

Tourist: Hey, could you tell us where the best wedding chapel is up here?
Me: What are you looking to do there?
Tourist: Ummm....get married.
Me: Ohhhh....
Tourist: Yeah, we kind of need to find a good one.
Me: So, you guys just met up here?
Tourist: Oh, no. We've been together almost 2 years. Just came up here to get married and have our honeymoon.
Me: Oh, so you didn't research wedding chapels before you came?
Tourist: No. We planned everything else like restaurants and attractions. But we didn't research wedding chapels.
Me: Oh. Gotcha. Those other things are much more important anyway.
Tourist: Haha.
Me: Seriously. They are expensive.
Tourist: No, our wedding is by far the most important part of the trip!
Me: More than eating?
Tourist: Ummm...of course.
Me: But you would starve. That would make the wedding uncomfortable.
Tourist: Oooo K. So, anyway, which one is known as the best?
Me: Do you want to wear costumes in the wedding?
Tourist: No. Not at all.
Me: Do you need a caterer?
Tourist: Ummm, no. It's just the 2 of us.
Me: Flowers?
Tourist: No.
Me: Flower Girl?
Tourist: No flowers, remember?
Me: Oh yeah, right. So, anyway, I don't know what to tell you.
Tourist: Oh. Then why all the questions?
Me: So I could give you a more informed answer.
Tourist: You didn't even give us an answer!!!
Me: That's probably because I'm uninformed.
Tourist: Huh?
Me: What?
Tourist: Never mind.
Me: Oh, so you're not getting married now?

#9 BEARS AND PANCAKES

Tourist: Hi man. How are ya?

Me: I'm really, really great. How about you?

Tourist: Oh good man. Very good.

Me: What can I do for ya?

Tourist: Well, I just had a real general question.

Me: That's good. I tend to give very vague answers.

Tourist: Oh haha, got it.

Me: So what do ya need?

Tourist: Well, I was just wondering what you are known for around here?

Me: Bears and Pancakes.

Tourist: So Gatlinburg is just known for bears and pancakes?

Me: Ohhhhh, no. I thought you asked what I was known for.

Tourist: (walks away briskly)

#10 WHOOPEE CUSHION

Tourist: Hi.
Me: Hi.
Tourist: Is there a good Arcade around here?
Me: To do what?
Tourist: Play games.
Me: Do you want to win tickets so you can win little Whoopee Cushions?
Tourist: Ummm, no. We don't really care about that.
Me: Why not? I like Whoopee Cushions.
Tourist: Yeah, we just want to play games.
Me: What kind of games?
Tourist: Any kind really. Shooting, racing games, whatever is cool.
Me: I like games too.
Tourist: Yeah great. So where do you go play?
Me: I don't.
Tourist: You just said you liked games?!
Me: I also said I like little Whoopee Cushions.
Tourist: Ok fine. Then where do you go to play games and win little Whoopee Cushions?
Me: I thought you said you didn't care about the little Whoopee Cushions.
Tourist: We don't.
Me: Oh.
Tourist: So Where??
Me: Whoopee Cushion.
Tourist: Huh?
Me: I like saying Whoopee Cushion.
Tourist: Ugh!!!!
Me: Ok, fine. I'll stop saying that.. Even though I don't want to stop.
Tourist: Thanks.
Me: You're very welcome.
Tourist: So, seriously…where do you go to play?
Me: I can't tell you that.
Tourist: (extremely frustrated) And why not?
Me: Because I'll mess up and say Whoopee Cushion and I promised I wouldn't.
Tourist: I've had enough of this.
Me: It's across the street.
Tourist: What is?
Me: The Whoopee Cushion place.

I TRAVEL TO SEE AND EXPERIENCE NEW THINGS. IT ALSO GIVES ME A GREAT OPPORTUNITY TO ASK STUPID QUESTIONS WITH NO REPERCUSSIONS.

~EVERY TOURIST EVER~

#11 SKIING

Tourist: Hey, do you know if the skiing up here is good?

Me: Define good.

Tourist: Big slopes...fast hills.

Me: I would think too big a slope would be highly difficult for a boat.

Tourist: No, snow!

Me: Definitely don't see a boat going on snow.

Tourist: (perturbed) I mean snow ski.

Me: Yeah, that makes more sense.

Tourist: So?

Me: I don't ski.

Tourist: Have you heard anything about skiing here though?

Me: Yes.

Tourist: And?

Me: It's available.

Tourist: That's it?!

Me: No.

Tourist: (steaming) Well????

Me: It's cold. Also, you should wear different clothes. You will get wet. Also, use those stick things to stop.

Tourist: You have absolutely been no help at all.

Me: That was absolutely my intention.

#12 THE PARADE

Tourist: Excuse me, what time does the parade start?
Me: Huh? It's Tuesday. In February. What parade?
Tourist: I don't know. Someone said there was a parade.
Me: Who did you talk to?
Tourist: Another couple at a restaurant.
Me: Did the guy have brown hair?
Tourist: I can't remember. Why?
Me: No reason.
Tourist: Oh, ok. So, there isn't a parade today?
Me: There might be. Sometimes these people who live in the mountains do random parades in town. There isn't a schedule. They just show up with floats made out of tree branches. They usually have animals with them.
Tourist: Ohhhh. Maybe that's what that couple was talking about?
Me: Ummm…yeah, must have been. Everyone around here knows about the hillbilly mountain parades.
Tourist: Are they fun to watch?
Me: Well, they are definitely different. Instead of throwing candy, they toss Acorns into the crowd. Really, really hurts.
Tourist: That sounds very odd!
Me: It is very odd.
Tourist: What kind of animals do they bring? Bobcats? Foxes?
Me: Chihuahuas mostly.
Tourist: Huh?
Me: Chihuahuas mostly.
Tourist: I heard you the first time, but that sounds really strange.
Me: They are Mountain Chihuahuas.
Tourist: Now we have to see this!!!
Me: You shouldn't.
Tourist: Why not?
Me: The Chihuahuas sometimes get loose from the float and start biting people in the crowd while fetching the acorns.
Tourist: Oh, that's horrible!!
Me: Yeah, I know. I think they should stop having the parades. The Mountain people are out of control.
Tourist: So how many of these Mountain people come to town?
Me: Like 3.
Tourist: That's all?

The Parade Continued....

Me: Yep. One Float. 3 Dudes. 2 Mountain Chihuahuas.
Tourist: And they call that a parade?
Me: They don't, but I do.
Tourist: And why is that?
Me: Well, it's actually just some rednecks who live up that hill and they come to town and drive an old crappy car. They are always "parading" around, so I just call it a parade.
Tourist: Seriously? You just totally wasted our time with that story?
Me: You call it a waste of time. I call it fantastic storytelling.

#13 THE GAMBLERS

Tourist: Hello.
Me: Hello.
Tourist: Is there a place to Gamble around here?
Me: Are you a professional?
Tourist: Haha oh no. Just for fun.
Me: I bet.
Tourist: Bet what?
Me: Oh, we are gambling now I see.
Tourist: Huh?
Me: Sorry. I just confused myself.
Tourist: So is there a casino or not?
Me: Not here. It's over the mountain.
Tourist: Which way?
Me: To the casino?
Tourist: Ummm….yeah.
Me: Turn around. See the mountains?
Tourist: Yes.
Me: It's over there. On the other side.
Tourist: Well how do you get there from here?
Me: You drive up the mountain. Then you drive down the mountain.
Tourist: No, I mean how do you get to the road to drive over the mountain?
Me: I'll flip you for it.
Tourist: That doesn't even make sense.
Me: I like to gamble too.
Tourist: I'm sure someone else can tell us then.
Me: I bet they can't.
Tourist: Really? You're the only person here who knows how to get there?
Me: I'm the only person here who will give you the wrong directions.
Tourist: I gathered that.
Me: So do you want me to tell you how to get there?
Tourist: No!!! You just said you were going to give us the wrong directions!!
Me: That is true.
Tourist: Does that guy know?
Me: That guy doesn't know anything. He's boring anyway.
Tourist: At least we'll get where we want to go.

THE GAMBLERS CONTINUED.....

Me: I doubt it. I once asked him where a good place to eat was and he didn't even acknowledge me.
Tourist: Really? He looks nice.
Me: Well, I did yell it across the street, and a Fire truck was blaring it's sirens, so he really never heard me.
Tourist: This is a waste of time.
Me: I could have told you that.

#14 SIRENS

TOURIST: HEY, WHAT'S UP WITH THE FIRETRUCK SIRENS?
ME: WHAT DO YOU MEAN?
TOURIST: WHY ARE THEY SO LOUD?
ME: I KNOW RIGHT? IT'S REALLY ANNOYING. I THINK THEY SHOULD PUT IT ON VIBRATE WHILE IN PUBLIC LIKE I HAVE TO DO WITH MY CELL PHONE. IT'S VERY RUDE.
TOURIST: WHAT?
ME: I TURN MY RINGER OFF ON MY PHONE. THEY SHOULD SILENCE THEIR SIRENS.
TOURIST: THAT WOULD DEFEAT THE POINT.
ME: WHAT POINT?
TOURIST: ALERTING PEOPLE TO MOVE OUT OF THE WAY.
ME: OH, YEAH...I GUESS YOU ARE RIGHT.
TOURIST: IT'S JUST WAY TOO LOUD.
ME: I THINK THEY PROBABLY DO THAT ON PURPOSE.
TOURIST: WHY?
ME: SOME PEOPLE ARE JUST STUPID YOU KNOW.
TOURIST: I GUESS. YOU GET A LOT OF STUPID QUESTIONS UP HERE I BET.
ME: APPARENTLY YOU HAVE NO IDEA.
TOURIST: HUH?
ME: NOTHING.
TOURIST: WHAT'S THE DUMBEST QUESTION ANYONE HAS EVER ASKED YOU UP HERE?
ME: YOU REALLY WANT ME TO ANWER THAT?
TOURIST: YES! (LEANING IN) WHY, IS IT DIRTY?
ME: HAHAHA NOPE.
TOURIST: THEN TELL ME! I'M VERY CURIOUS.
ME: WELL, IT WAS ABOUT BEARS.
TOURIST: WHAT DID THEY ASK?
ME: NOTHING IMPORTANT.
TOURIST: OH WELL I GUESS YOU AREN'T GOING TO TELL ME.

SIRENS CONTINUED.....

ME: HEY, AT LEAST YOU ARE PROBABLY IN THE TOP TEN!
TOURIST: TOP TEN WHAT?
ME: DUMBEST QUESTIONS. THAT FIRETRUCK THING WAS PRICELESS!
TOURIST: YOU THOUGHT THAT WAS A DUMB QUESTION?
ME: NO.
TOURIST: OH. GOOD.
ME: I KNOW IT WAS A DUMB QUESTION!

#15 BATHROOMS

TOURIST: HEY YOU...IS THERE A BATHROOM CLOSE?
ME: YES.
TOURIST: WHERE IS IT?
ME: PUBLIC OR PRIVATE?
TOURIST: I DON'T CARE!!!
ME: WELL, I WOULDN'T GO TO THE BATHROOM IN PUBLIC IF I WERE YOU.
TOURIST: HUH?
ME: WOULD BE EMBARRASSING WITH ALL THESE PEOPLE WATCHING.
TOURIST: ARE YOU SERIOUS?
ME: YES! I WOULD SERIOUSLY BE EMBARRASSED GOING TO THE BATHROOM IN FRONT OF ALL THESE PEOPLE!
TOURIST: GEEZ. IS THERE AN ACTUAL BATHROOM CLOSE?
ME: HOW CLOSE?
TOURIST: ANYWHERE!
ME: THERE HAS TO BE.
TOURIST: WHAT DO YOU MEAN NOW?
ME: I'D BE SURPRISED IF THERE ARE NO BATHROOMS AROUND. I WOULDN'T WANT TO BE AROUND ALL THESE PEOPLE IF THERE WEREN'T ANY BATHROOMS. ESPECIALLY IF THEY HAD YOUR IDEA OF GOING IN PUBLIC.
TOURIST: (AGITATED) YEAH THAT WOULD BE COMMON SENSE.
ME: I KNOW IT IS.
TOURIST: SO, YOU DON'T HAVE ANY IDEA?
ME: NOPE.
TOURIST: WHERE DO YOU USE THE BATHROOM THEN?
ME: I HAVE A PRIVATE ONE.
TOURIST: CAN I USE IT?
ME: I'M SORRY. SEE THE SIGN? IT SAYS NO PUBLIC RESTROOMS.
TOURIST: OH.

BATHROOMS CONTINUED....

ME: I NEED TO MAKE A NEW SIGN TO ALSO SAY "NO PRIVATE RESTROOMS EITHER."
TOURIST: THAT'S JUST STUPID.
ME: IT MIGHT BE STUPID BUT IT MAKES SENSE.
TOURIST: NO IT DOESN'T.
ME: YES IT DOES.
TOURIST: SO WHERE IS THE NEAREST PUBLIC RESTROOM?
ME: WELL, SEE THE SIGN 5 FEET FROM YOUR FACE? IT SAYS PUBLIC RESTROOMS THIS WAY.
TOURIST: OH. YEAH, I SEE IT.
ME: I WOULDN'T GO THERE THOUGH, IT'S NASTY.
TOURIST: HOW DO YOU KNOW? YOU HAVE A RESTROOM HERE.
ME: REMEMBER, IT'S PRIVATE. AND IT'S NOT MINE. IT'S MY WIFE'S.

#16 TENNIS

tourist: hello sir! could you help us with something?
me: sure, unless it involves moving heavy objects. my back hurts.
tourist: oh i'm sorry, did you pull a muscle?
me: oh, no. i'm just extremely lazy.
tourist: oh. well, it's nothing like that.
me: good. then i might help you.
tourist: ohhhh….k. well, is there a good place to play tennis around here?
me: like with rackets and stuff?
tourist: yes.
me: are you not on vacation?
tourist: yes we are.
me: then why in the world would you want to exercise?
tourist: because we love to play tennis.
me: i love to play basketball, but when i'm on vacation i try not to move at all.
tourist: well, we try to stay fit.
me: see, once again, opposites. i try to stay unfit. i'm quite good at it.
tourist: i see.
me: how, i'm not even standing up?
tourist: ok then. so, is there a place to play tennis or not?
me: did you bring your own net?
tourist: of course not!
me: ok. that eliminates playing in the road or on the sidewalk.
tourist: yeah, we need an actual tennis court.
me: ohhhh…gotcha.
tourist: so?
me: i have no clue.
tourist: oh well, we can ask around then.
me: you can ask everybody. they will tell you the same thing though.
tourist: tell us they don't know where a court is?
me: no. they will tell you that they know that i don't know where a court is.
tourist: that doesn't really make any sense.
me: they will tell you that as well.

#17 THE CROSSWALK

Me: Boy, you barely made it!
Tourist: I know! Hey, what's up with these crosswalks?
Me: (here we go) What do you mean?
Tourist: I don't understand how they work.
Me: Yeah, they are extremely confusing.
Tourist: So, how do you know when to walk?
Me: Oh yeah, that's the hard part. Well, there is a sign that lights up at the other side of the street. It will say "Walk."
Tourist: Oh.
Me: Yeah.
Tourist: What about the ones that don't have signs and are not at lights? There seem to be a lot of those.
Me: Yeah, those are the fun ones.
Tourist: What do you mean?
Me: Locals call it "Pedestrian Games."
Tourist: Why?
Me: Cuz they wait for you to cross then "Bam!"
Tourist: Really?
Me: Yes.
Tourist: That's horrible!!
Me: Unless you are the driver.
Tourist: Have you hit someone?
Me: No.
Tourist: Oh.
Me: I usually swerve.
Tourist: Why don't you just stop?
Me: Because you can hit more people when you swerve on the sidewalk.
Tourist: What????
Me: I'm just kidding.
Tourist: Whew. I figured. At least I hoped you were.
Me: I do like to throw things at them though.
Tourist: Ok, come on now.
Me: Throw something at you now?
Tourist: No, you are still just joking around.

THE CROSSWALK CONTINUED…..

Me: Ok, I'm joking. Well, just be careful at the crosswalks. We have a lot of Goth people up here.
Tourist: What does that matter?
Me: It doesn't. I was just letting you know.
Tourist: Okie dokie then, I guess I'll see you later.
Me: Probably. Unless you get hit.

#18 THE BROCHURE

Tourist: Hi, do you know where I can get a brochure?
Me: A brochure for what?
Tourist: Anything!
Me: Wow, you collect them too?
Tourist: Brochures?
Me: Yeah (acting outrageously excited) I got a 2007 one from a cool Amusement park in Pennsylvania. Lots of colors. Worth like 9 cents!
Tourist: That's odd. You being for real?
Me: Yeah. Matter of fact, will you do me a favor?
Tourist: Ummm...like what?
Me: While you are walking around, will you look for a 2009 purple brochure?
Tourist: Ok....why?
Me: I hear there may have been a misprint. Could be worth literally over $.10.
Tourist: That's literally not worth it.
Me: Well, combined with the dollar off coupon attached, it's well worth it.
Tourist: Ohhhhh.....I get it. You use them for discounts?
Me: Hahaha! Yeah right? And tear a mint brochure? I think not!
Tourist: I've never heard of this, but thanks. Have a good one.
Me: (yelling) Ok...don't forget! Purple 2009!!!!

#19 THE ADULT STORE

Tourist: Is that "Couples Only" place across the street an Adult Store?
Me: I don't follow.
Tourist: Adult Store.
Me: You are shopping for Adults?
Tourist: No, that couples store across the street. Is it for Adults only?
Me: Who wants to know?
Tourist: (yelling) Me!!!
Me: Shhhhhh....not so loud. I get embarrassed easily talking about that kind of stuff.
Tourist: (angry) So...is...it?
Me: No.
Tourist: It's not an Adult Store?
Me: It can be.
Tourist: I'll just go see for myself!
Me: You can't do that.
Tourist: WHY NOT!!!!
Me: Because it's for couples only.

YEAH, I KNOW IT'S A CLOWN. TRYING TO KEEP THIS BOOK PG YOU KNOW.

#20 THE CHAIR LIFT

Tourist: Hey, is the chair lift romantic?
Me: Depends. Do you want it to be?
Tourist: Ummmm...yeah, that's why I asked.
Me: Oh. Gotcha. Well some people ask if It's easy to push off their significant other, so I was making sure.
Tourist: People really ask you that?
Me: All the time. I say yes.
Tourist: Wow! That's crazy! How could someone do something like that!?
Me: Well, first you lift the bar, then firmly place hand on their back....
Tourist:(cutting me off) haha, that's funny.
Me: My wife didn't think it was funny...I mean, at least it didn't sound like laughter from up there.
Tourist:(rolling eyes) Ok thanks.
Me: Good luck! (yelling) DON'T FORGET TO LIFT BAR FIRST!!! OTHERWISE SHE WILL JUST BE ANGRY!

If you ask me for hiking directions, then there is a very good chance you are in for a helicopter rescue.

~Alex Stokes~

#21 VALENTINE'S COUPLE

Tourist: Excuse me, but what would you recommend for the most romantic restaurant for Valentine's day?
Me: Well, first of all I commend you for bringing your wife to America's #1 voted romantic city.
Tourist: Really? It's #1?
Me: Well, when I said America, I meant the County. Also, when I said voted, I meant my opinion.
Tourist: (laughing)
Me: It's not funny.
Tourist: Oh. So any recommendations?
Me: Do you need candles, wine, romantic atmosphere, good food?
Tourist: Sure!
Me: Then I don't know.
Tourist: Oh.
Me: You Like pancakes?
Tourist: Yes, but not what I had in mind.
Me: You are being too picky then.
Tourist: Well, I guess I'll ask someone else.
Me: Ok. Come back in 5 minutes and more than likely I'll be someone else. Happens often.
I'm what they call...
Tourist : (cutting me off) multiple personalities?
Me: No. Bored.

#22 THE HAUNTED HOUSE

Tourist: Man, that haunted house is scary!
Me: Really? They should put that on a sign so you will know.
Tourist: Know what?
Me: That it's scary. Not cool to find out the hard way.
Tourist: But it says haunted house, so I knew.
Me: Oh, gotcha. Then why did you tell me?
Tourist: I figured you would want to know it's scary.
Me: Actually, I already knew it was scary.
Tourist: Oh, you've been?
Me: No. I heard you screaming from across the street "Oh my that haunted house is freaking scary!!!"
Tourist: (Laughing) You heard that?
Me: No. I just said that I heard that.

#23 TAMALES

Tourist: Excuse me, but where is the best place to go eat Mexican.
Me: Food?
Tourist: Yes.
Me: Hmmm...Probably the Pasta place.
Tourist: (confused) That's Italian.
Me: I know.
Tourist: Soooo....why would I go there?
Me: Because there is a busboy there named Joey, and his grandmother makes really good authentic Tamales. He usually has some in his car.
Tourist: Ok, first of all this is ridiculous, and anyway I don't like Tamales. Anywhere else?
Me: Are you sure you want me to answer that?
Tourist: (walks away)

More Clowns. I couldn't find pictures of Tamales.

#24 PIGEONS

Tourist: Hello there.
Me: Hello there.
Tourist: Oh, could you tell me what is going on with all the pigeons here?
Me: Oh sure.
Tourist: Great.
Me: This town used to be, hundreds of years ago, a giant post office.
Tourist: Huh?
Me: Yeah, that's why there are so many pigeons. They are descendants.
Tourist: What in the world are you talking about?
Me: Oh, sorry. In the 1800's this town was well known as a Mail Hub in the Southeast. Hence all the pigeons.
Tourist: This is the funniest story I've heard in a while.
Me: It's not a story. Read a brochure about it.
Tourist: Are you serious?
Me: Yeah. Only thing is this generation of pigeons is nothing like their ancestors.
Tourist: What do you mean?
Me: They are lazy and rarely fly. Just hassle tourists all day. They are bum pigeons.
Tourist: Man you are hilarious!
Me: Do you see me laughing?
Tourist: If I went and asked someone else about this they would laugh at me.
Me: Yes. Yes they would. Just ignore them.
Tourist: They would probably tell me to ignore you and anything you say.
Me: That would be a mistake.
Tourist: And why is that?
Me: I know things they don't.
Tourist: And how do you know all this stuff?
Me: Because I talk to the pigeons.
Tourist: Oh man, you really are nuts!
Me: I didn't say they talked back. Everyone knows pigeons can't talk.
Tourist: Is this a game you are playing with me?
Me: Yes, and I'm winning.

#25 CAMEL RIDES

Tourist: Hey! Do they have Camel rides in the mountains?
Me: Camels?
Tourist: Yeah.
Me: Yes.
Tourist: Oh cool! Where?
Me: Camels?
Tourist: Ummm...yeah. You already said they had Camel rides.
Me: Yeah, I remember saying that.
Tourist: So?
Me: Camels, right?
Tourist: Yes!!!
Me: There are not any Camels around here.
Tourist: You said there were.
Me: I thought you said Mammals.
Tourist: No, Camels.
Me: A Camel is a Mammal.
Tourist: I know.
Me: Then why did you ask?
Tourist: Ask what?
Me: About the Llamas.
Tourist: No! I....said.....Camels!!!
Me: That's just ridiculous.
Tourist: What, Camels?
Me: Yes. Everyone knows Camels don't live here.
Tourist: That's why I asked.
Me: But I said everyone knows.
Tourist: What are you insinuating?
Me: I'm not burning anything.
Tourist: Goodbye.
Me: Fine. I'm not going to tell you where they have Llama rides now.

#26 GAS STATIONS

Tourist: Hey, where can I find the nearest Gas Station?
Me: There aren't any.
Tourist: What do you mean there are no Gas Stations?
Me: Seriously. There aren't any.
Tourist: Then what do people do?
Me: They either get gas in the previous town or they just drive until they run out.
Tourist: For real?
Me: For Realio. By the way, I think I just made up the word for Realio. I think.
Tourist: So you are telling me people just run out of gas up here all the time?
Me: I guess so. Look at that parking lot. It's full of cars. Nobody driving them!! Kind of odd don't you think?
Tourist: Ummm, no. It's a parking lot.
Me: You call it a parking lot. I call it an out of gas lot.
Tourist: That's just stupid.
Me: I think that park bench is stupid.
Tourist: What?
Me: I didn't' want to call you stupid. So, I looked at you but said Park Bench.
Tourist: So you are calling me stupid?
Me: Is your name park bench?
Tourist: (very angry) According to your previous comment then yes!
Me: That's an odd name to have.
Tourist: I'm very angry right now.
Me: Hold on. You're on hidden camera!!
Tourist: Really? Is this a television prank? Hahaha! You got me!!
Me: No. I just have a hidden camera.
Tourist: What? Is that even legal?
Me: I'm just kidding. You're not on camera.
Tourist: Oh….now I'm confused.
Me: That you are.
Tourist: Is this some kind of stunt?
Me: Do you see a skateboard?
Tourist: Huh?
Me: You said stunt. I said skateboard. Follow along please.
Tourist: Forget it.
Me: Ok. By the way, Gas Station 1 mile down the road.

#27 ROD RUN

Tourist: Hey! Can you tell me something?
Me: I can tell you a lot of things. I'm like super smart.
Tourist: No man. I was just wondering what all these Old Timey Cars are doing here.
Me: It's called a Rod Run.
Tourist: What's that?
Me: It's where a bunch of people from all over bring their old fixed up cars.
Tourist: What do they do?
Me: They sit in Lawn chairs.
Tourist: And do what?
Me: Sit.
Tourist: That's it?
Me: Yes.
Tourist: So why all the cars then?
Me: They are basically just eye candy.
Tourist: Eye candy?
Me: Yep. They sit in the lawn chairs and stare at the cars as they drive by.
Tourist: Who's driving the cars if everyone is sitting in lawn chairs?
Me: Nobody. Most of them are remote control I think.
Tourist: Yeah man that's not true at all.
Me: Then you explain it to me. There are thousands of people sitting in lawn chairs. More people than there are cars. The cars go like 3 miles an hour.
Tourist: I'm sure somebody is driving them.
Me: I personally believe they are Old Timey Ghost cars. That's what others around here believe too.
Tourist: You are messed up.
Me: No. It's true. Like Super true.
Tourist: That doesn't make any sense at all.
Me: You are the one who doesn't believe.
Tourist: Now you are just confusing me.
Me: Ok. Here's what you do. Go buy a lawn chair and sit on the side of the road.
Tourist: And do what?

ROD RUN CONTINUED…..

Me: Look at the cars as they go by. I bet either no one is driving them or there is a skeleton in the driver's seat.
Tourist: Skeleton? Come on man seriously?
Me: Ummm….have you seen the people in the lawn chairs? Matter of fact, have you seen the lawn chairs? They are those old style mesh woven ones. All skeleton people I tell you.
Tourist: You have some imagination.
Me: No. Well, yes. But the Ghost Rod Runs are real. Trust me..

#28 THE HOTEL

Tourist: Sir, we seem to have lost our hotel.
Me: I know.
Tourist: What? What do you mean you know?
Me: I'm an information booth, remember?
Tourist: What in the world?
Me: I pretty much know everything around here.
Tourist: That doesn't even have anything to do with our problem.
Me: Drinking problem?
Tourist: What???!!!
Me: Sorry. Sometimes I'm wrong. Ok, so you lost your hotel right?
Tourist: I'm inclined to not talk to you anymore.
Me: That would be a terrible, terrible mistake.
Tourist: How so?
Me: I know where your hotel is.
Tourist: Oh really?
Me: Yep. It's in town.
Tourist: Oh you're a real genius.
Me: Awww, thank you! But I'm really not as smart as you claim.
Tourist: (super angry) Ok hot shot….where's our hotel then?
Me: It's on the Main street.
Tourist: Oh wow. Brilliant.
Me: Thanks again!
Tourist: Seriously, where is it?
Me: Look, I'm going to be honest with you. I highly doubt your hotel has moved Sir.
Tourist: Wow. You are a really frustrating person to talk to.
Me: Yeah, I hear that a lot. I don't mind when people brag about me though.
Tourist: Who is your boss?
Me: I don't have one. Well, I do, but he doesn't like talking to me either.
Tourist: I don't blame him.
Me: Yeah, you shouldn't blame him. He had nothing at all to do with the disappearance of your hotel.
Tourist: Unbelievable.
Me: I know right! An entire Hotel vanishing is unbelievable!

#29 CHRISTMAS DECORATIONS

Tourist: Excuse me, can I ask you a question?
Me: No. Go ahead.
Tourist: Ok. Do you know when they take down the Christmas decorations?
Me: I don't know what you mean.
Tourist: There are snowflake lights on the traffic poles.
Me: I'm not following.
Tourist: Giant snowflakes on the poles.
Me: Yes, I know that.
Tourist: When do they take them down?
Me: They don't.
Tourist: Why not?
Me: Because we need traffic lights for cars.
Tourist: No, I mean just the snowflakes!
Me: That's silly.
Tourist: Do you not understand what I'm saying?
Me: What I don't understand, sir, is why there are snowflakes on the traffic poles.
Tourist: Nooo!!! Just tell me!!!!
Me: Tell you what?
Tourist: What I asked you before?
Me: About the bathrooms?
Tourist: That was the woman in front of me!
Me: Oh yeah. I remember.
Tourist: So?
Me: I honestly forgot what we were talking about.
Tourist: Snowflakes on the traffic poles!
Me: Oh yeah. You know what I've always wondered?
Tourist: What?
Me: Why they are up there. You have any idea?

#30 PUNK TEENAGERS

Tourists: Dude, is there anything fun to do around here?
Me: Of course! Legal or illegal?
Tourists: Dude....Ummmm...illegal! Can you hook us up?
Me: Sure can.
Tourists: Sweet!
Me: Ok, see that blue car by that dumpster?
Tourists: (excited) Oh yeah man.
Me: Ok. Slowly walk up to that car.
Tourists: Ok and do what?
Me: Look over your shoulder, both ways.
Tourists: Of course. Then what.
Me: Smash the window out.
Tourists: Huh?
Me: It's illegal to do that. Enjoy.

SHORT AND STUPID

Me: Where you guys from?
Husband tourist: Alabama.
Me: Oh, what part?
Wife Tourist: Missouri.
Me: Great! Welcome to North Dakota!

#31 CROWDED

Tourist: Hey why is it so crowded here?
Me: Apparently because there is not enough room for everyone.
Tourist: What?
Me: I think that's what crowded means. I can look it up to be sure.
Tourist: Yeah no duh.
Me: I like it when people say "No Duh." That's funny.
Tourist: So anyway why are all these people here?
Me: Why are you here?
Tourist: Vacation.
Me: Oh, now that's weird!!!
Tourist: What do you mean weird?
Me: All the rest of the people are here for a giant cornhole tournament. Not vacation.
Tourist: Ohhhh….I knew it was something like that.
Me: Oh really?
Tourist: Yeah, I figured there couldn't be that many people coming to a place like this.
Me: So, you don't have the internet where you are from do you?
Tourist: Of course I do.
Me: Did you research this place?
Tourist: No.
Me: (changing directions again) Oh. Well, we are well known for cornhole tournaments. The only reason people go into the mountains anymore is to chop down large trees to carve cornhole boards out of.
Tourist: Really? That's strange. I've seen a TON of cars going into the mountains.
Me: I know. Lots of cornholers.
Tourist: Is that legal to chop down trees in the mountains?
Me: Nobody knows. Nobody cares. It's all about the money.
Tourist: Money? Is cornhole profitable?
Me: For the bean bag makers, yes.
Tourist: Wow! This is fascinating!

CROWDED CONTINUED....

Me: You do know I'm making all this up as I go along, right?
Tourist: Seriously?
Me: Yep. Funny huh?
Tourist: Not really.
Me: I was laughing on the inside the whole time. Now I'm laughing on the outside.
Tourist: I'm not laughing at all.
Me: What can I do to make you laugh then?
Tourist: Nothing at this point.
Me: I should of picked a different point then.

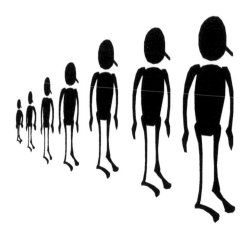

MORE SHORT AND STUPID

Tourist: Can you believe the nerve of some of the businesses up here that only take cash?
Me: Well, give them credit. That means they are doing SOOO well they don't have to take cards.
Tourist: Well, I guess. Can you break a $50?
Me: Sorry, we don't take cash.
Tourist: (screaming)WHAT!!!!!!?????
Me: We aren't doing that well.

#32 SNOW ON CARS

Tourist: Excuse me, but I was wondering something.
Me: It's not true.
Tourist: Huh?
Me: What you were wondering about me. It's not true.
Tourist: I don't know what you are talking about.
Me: Forget we ever had this conversation then.
Tourist: Can I still ask you a question?
Me: Sure. What is it?
Tourist: Ok. How is there snow on the mountains, and on some cars down here, but none on the ground down here?
Me: (Wow)Depends on who you ask. Most round these parts believe people drive cars up the mountain, get covered in snow, then come back down the mountain.
Tourist: And what do other people believe?
Me: Aliens.

#33 CAJUN FOOD

Tourist: Excuse me, where is the best place to get Cajun food?
Me: I think New Orleans.
Tourist: No, I meant around here.
Me: New Orleans isn't really close to here.
Tourist: No, Cajun food around here. Where is the best place?
Me: Ohhhh, you should have said that!
Tourist: I did.
Me: That is correct.
Tourist: Whew…ok, so any suggestions?
Me: No.
Tourist: Oh well.
Me: I mean yes.
Tourist: Soooo….
Me: No, it doesn't start with "soooo…"
Tourist: Man come on.
Me: I'm sorry, but I can't go with you.
Tourist: (agitated) Are you trying to mess with my head?
Me: No, I don't have to try. It just comes naturally.
Tourist: Well, you are definitely good at it.
Me: Thank you!
Tourist: Not really a compliment.
Me: Well, maybe not in your circle of friends. My friends like it though.
Tourist: They like it when you mess with them?
Me: No. They like it when I mess with people like you and then tell them all about it.
Tourist: That makes sense.
Me: That's the first thing you've said this whole conversation that made sense.
Tourist: Huh?
Me: Never mind. So, you were asking about good Italian food? Just down the street on the left or the right.
Tourist: Yeah thanks for nothing.
Me: You're welcome for something.

Woof.

~Every Tourist's Dog Ever.~

#34 I DON'T GET IT

Tourist: Hello there! How are you?
Me: I'm great! How are you?
Tourist: Good. Hey, I've got a question you might be able to help me with.
Me: Sure! Go ahead.
Tourist: I've been walking up and down the strip, and I can't really tell what is the big deal about this town.
Me: What do you mean?
Tourist: Why do so many people come here?
Me: Well, the mountains are a huge attraction!
Tourist: Oh, really? I haven't seen anyone hiking.
Me: Nobody hikes on the strip.
Tourist: Even when I was in the mountains, I didn't see anyone hiking.
Me: What part of the mountains were you in?
Tourist: (pointing) That part.
Me: Oh. Yeah, nobody hikes there.
Tourist: We did.
Me: When I said nobody, I meant very few people.
Tourist: You should have said that then.
Me: But I didn't say that.
Tourist: I know.
Me: This is stupid.
Tourist: What is stupid?
Me: This conversation.
Tourist: Why is that?
Me: Are you just going to keep going? You are a funny little man.
Tourist: I'm just trying to figure out why all these people are here.
Me: I'll tell you a secret.
Tourist: Great.
Me: The people who are here don't even know why they are here.
Tourist: Now that makes more sense!
Me: It does?
Tourist: Yes.
Me: Hmmm. Interesting.
Tourist: What's interesting?
Me: I usually don't make any sense.
Tourist: Oh.
Me: Yeah. So, anyway, why are YOU here?
Tourist: I don't really know.
Me: Wow. I really did make sense.

SHORT AND STUPID

Tourist: Hey, do you know why it's raining?
Me: Do I look like a meteorologist?
Tourist: No, just wondering if you knew.
Me: I didn't pay attention to that part in school.
Tourist: No, I just wanted to know from a local stand point.
Me: I went to school locally, and I still didn't pay attention, and I still don't know.
Tourist: No! Why is it raining here!?
Me: You do realize that is one of the dumbest questions ever, right?
Tourist: How is that?
Me: Seriously, go ask your wife how stupid that question is.
Tourist: She's the one who told me to ask you.
Me: How are you guys getting home? I'm worried for you guys.

#35 THE FOG MACHINE

Tourist: Hi!!!
Me: Heeeeyyyyyy!!!!
Tourist: Could you tell me something?
Me: I hate Tuna Fish. Like really bad.
Tourist: Huh?
Me: Oh. It's all I could think of to tell you.
Tourist: Oh. Haha. So anyway, where exactly do they turn on the Fog in the Mountains?
Me: Oh no you didn't.
Tourist: Didn't what?
Me: You are asking about the Mountain Fog machine?
Tourist: Yes. It's really neat how they make it look so pretty in the trees.
Me: Oh I know. The little man who runs it is like an artist.
Tourist: So where is he located?
Me: Underground.
Tourist: Figures.
Me: Yeah.
Tourist: Is it expensive to make?
Me: I don't think so. I've heard it's like real air.
Tourist: I guess the machine needs lots of power though.
Me: I guess. Also add in all the cost for incense..
Tourist: Incense?
Me: Oh yeah. That's what gives it the Smokey look. It's from India or Indiana. I can't remember.
Tourist: Hmmmm. I would have never thought that.
Me: Are you sure?

#36 TELL US A JOKE

Tourist: Hey man. That guy across the street said you were a Stand Up Comedian.
Me: You could call it that yes.
Tourist: Tell us a joke!
Me: I can't.
Tourist: Why not?
Me: Because there are kids here.
Tourist: It won't bother them. Trust me. Go ahead.
Me: But it will bother me.
Tourist: Fine. Then take out the bad words.
Me: I can't.
Tourist: Why not?
Me: Because then it wouldn't make sense. Sentences need verbs and adjectives.
Tourist: Wow.
Me: I know right. I can't help it.

#37 DONUTS

Tourist: Hey where's the Donut place?
Me: You mean pancakes.
Tourist: No, I said Donuts.
Me: I said Pancakes.
Tourist: Why are you talking like that?
Me: Because you were rude.
Tourist: How was I rude?
Me: First of all, you just yelled a question at me.
Tourist: Sorry. I'm in a hurry.
Me: Second of all, you said Donuts, and I have a fear of Donuts.
Tourist: What in the?
Me: Yeah, since I was a kid. So you kind of scared me.
Tourist: You got scared because I yelled Donut?
Me: Well, that and your outfit.
Tourist: Huh?
Me: It's scary.
Tourist: I've been hiking!!
Me: To the Donut place?
Tourist: No, in the mountains!
Me: I hate to tell you this, but there aren't any Donut places in the Mountains.
Tourist: Yeah, I figured that out.
Me: So you DID go looking for one huh?
Tourist: Man you're weird.
Me: I would say I'm more handsome than weird. Either or.
Tourist: Well, I would disagree.
Me: Disagree with what? I said either or.
Tourist: What?
Me: Man you are confusing. You should eat a donut and get some sugar in you.
Tourist: I don't eat donuts.
Me: So you had a bad experience as a kid too?
Tourist: What?
Me: I give up. Turn around. There are donuts. Bye Bye.

#38 COUPONS

Tourist: Hello?
Me: Hi.
Tourist: I have this coupon for buy one get one free. Can I use this?
Me: Let me see. (looking at it.) Ummmm, no.
Tourist: Why not?
Me: Well, first of all, it's for a dinner entrée.
Tourist: And?
Me: Yeah, we are an attraction, not a restaurant.
Tourist: So?
Me: Well. Ok. Let me explain. No.
Tourist: I don't understand why I can't just use this coupon.
Me: I understand that you don't understand reality.
Tourist: What? That was just confusing.
Me: I'm pretty sure you were confused after I said Hi.
Tourist: You are being extremely rude.
Me: What do you expect? You are mad that you can't use a restaurant coupon at an attraction.
Tourist: It doesn't make sense!
Me: Ok. Scenario time. Let's just say….in a perfectly stupid world…that you could use any coupon at any place up here. Restaurants, attractions, gas stations, etc. As long as it was from this town, you could use it. Do you understand so far?
Tourist: Yes, I understand.
Me: Ok. Well, even in that perfectly stupid scenario, you still wouldn't be able to use your coupon.
Tourist: And why is that?
Me: Because it's a restaurant coupon from your hometown newspaper. In another state.
Tourist: Yes, I get that.
Me: Do I need to explain my scenario again? Or do I need to do a new scenario that is even dumber than the first one?
Tourist: Just forget it.
Me: Ok. One last question.
Tourist: What?
Me: Can I have your sweater?
Tourist: Huh? That's a stupid question!!
Me: Now we are even. Goodbye.

#39 DOG STROLLERS

Tourist: Hey, what's up with all the dogs in strollers up here?
Me: They are puppies.
Tourist: I know.
Me: Stupid isn't it?
Tourist: I didn't say that.
Me: You should have. I did.
Tourist: I just don't understand it.
Me: Of everything you have seen in this town THAT is what you don't understand?
Tourist: Well, I get the concept.
Me: I once saw a donkey in a stroller.
Tourist: Really?
Me: No.
Tourist: Oh.
Me: It was just an ugly puppy.
Tourist: (laughing) That's funny.
Me: I'm serious. It was really ugly.
Tourist: What breed was it?
Me: Well, it was actually a baby.

When I see her put that outfit on to go out in public, I remind myself "Hey, we don't know anybody here. It's ok."

~Female Tourist's Husbands~

TOP TWENTY ITEMS TOURISTS LOOK FOR IN THE MOUNTAINS

1. BEARS
2. DEER
3. WATERFALLS
4. CLOWNS
5. TREES
6. LEAVES
7. VIEWS
8. FERRIS WHEELS
9. BOBCATS
10. BIRDS
11. TRAILS
12. HIKING STICKS
13. ELEPHANTS
14. SQUIRRELS
15. SNAKES
16. BUGS
17. PANCAKES
18. WATER
19. FLOWERS
20. THE REST OF THEIR PARTY

#40 TAFFY

Tourist: I need taffy. Where can I get it?
Me: Hello. My name is Alex.
Tourist: What?
Me: Sorry. I didn't mean to use normal conversation.
Tourist: Oh.
Me: Yeah.
Tourist: So, where can I get some taffy?
Me: You like Root Beer?
Tourist: What does that have to do with taffy?
Me: They make Root Beer taffy.
Tourist: Oh. Gotcha. So where?
Me: Well, I think most of the Taffy places make Root Beer taffy.
Tourist: No, I meant where can I get some taffy.
Me: The taffy place.
Tourist: And where is that?
Me: Taffy.
Tourist: What?
Me: Sorry. I just like saying taffy.
Tourist: That's fine. Do you not know?
Me: Well, nobody really knows about taffy. It's probably one of the seven wonders of the world.
Tourist: What in the world are you talking about?
Me: Taffy.
Tourist: I know that. I meant what did you mean about the Seven wonders thing?
Me: I was almost joking about that part.
Tourist: Ok. I see this is going nowhere.
Me: That's how it starts.
Tourist: That's how what starts?
Me: The secret of taffy.
Tourist: Wow.
Me: I know right.
Tourist: You're an idiot.

#41 THE LOST CELL PHONE

Tourist: (panicking) Hey! Hey! Have you seen a cell phone?
Me: Yes. It's 2012.
Tourist: What?
Me: I've not only seen them, I've already had like 10 before.
Tourist: No!!!! I lost mine and I can't find it!
Me: So, let me get this straight. You lost your cell phone AND you can't find it? Which is it?
Tourist: Huh?
Me: You seem confused.
Tourist: I'm frustrated! I have a lot of important information on that phone!
Me: Yes, I know.
Tourist: Excuse me?
Me: I just meant most people keep important information on their cell phone. Don't act like I have it or anything. It's not like I've been going through all your pictures.
Tourist: How do I know you haven't?
Me: Because everybody trusts me. They probably shouldn't though.
Tourist: So now I'm confused.
Me: No.
Tourist: What?
Me: You were confused before.
Tourist: So, you haven't seen a cell phone. That's all I need to know.
Me: If that's all you need to know, then you must be really smart.
Tourist: Oh....my.....
Me: Are you getting mad at me?
Tourist: Yes.
Me: I'm sorry. Would it make you feel better if I said someone turned in your cell phone an hour ago?
Tourist: Yes, that would be wonderful!!!
Me: Gosh. I really wish I could have told you that. You would have been so excited!

#42 THE TALLEST TREE

Tourist: Hello there! How are you doing today?
Me: I'm great! Glad to finally meet someone normal!
Tourist: Haha I bet! I hope the question I'm going to ask you doesn't make me sound stupid!
Me: I'm sure it won't! Go ahead!
Tourist: Ok. So, I'm sure you probably know this. If I'm looking that way toward the mountains, could you point to the tallest tree for me?
Me: You do know that from here it's a long ways away.
Tourist: I know. I figured you probably knew though.
Me: No, I'm stumped.
Tourist: Darn.
Me: I made a joke and you missed it.
Tourist: Huh?
Me: I said stumped.
Tourist: (not laughing) Oh.
Me: It's ok. I tell my wife and kids I'm a comedian, but I think they know.
Tourist: Know what?
Me: That I know nothing about Trees.
Tourist: Ok. I guess.
Me: No, it's ok.
Tourist: So you have no idea?
Me: Oh....the tallest tree. That's right. Yeah, I think I know.
Tourist: Oh cool! Which one?
Me: (pointing aimlessly) The one with the initials TT on it. See that?
Tourist: Ummmm....there is no way we could see that from here.
Me: Hmmm. Strange.
Tourist: What's strange?
Me: Well, I thought you must have like supernatural powers. I guess you are just like all the tourists.
Tourist: Well I never!
Me: Obviously.

#43 WOLVES

Tourist: Hey! Man, I was wondering if you guys have a lot of wolves around here? I think we saw one.
Me: Was it black?
Tourist: No, Reddish.
Me: Ohhhh, I see.
Tourist: Do you think it was a wolf?
Me: Possibly. I've only seen one ever.
Tourist: What color was it?
Me: Reddish.
Tourist: Aha!!
Me: And blackish.
Tourist: Huh?
Me: And Whitish.
Tourist: Ok which was it?
Me: Well, Reddish body, Whitish Patches, Black Eyelids.
Tourist: Oh, so it was Reddish.
Me: And Blackish and Whitish.
Tourist: Ok yeah whatever.
Me: Seriously, it was creepy. I'd never seen a wolf look like that up close.
Tourist: How many wolves have you seen up close?
Me: Just that one. That's why I said I had never seen one look like that up close.
Tourist: Alrighty then.
Me: Glad you understand now.
Tourist: Do you understand?
Me: Not really.
Tourist: That's what I figured.
Me: Well, anyway, I saw that wolf just running down the strip.
Tourist: Doing what?
Me: Running.
Tourist: Running where?
Me: I didn't ask him. Anyway, unless he was an actual Wolfman, he wouldn't be able to talk back to me.
Tourist: Unbelievable. You are just gonna keep going aren't you?
Me: It depends.
Tourist: Depends on what?
Me: If you are still here. If you leave, I won't talk to you anymore.
Tourist: (Walks away.)

#44 ICE CREAM AND BIRDS

Tourist: Ok. So, this is going to sound like a strange question.
Me: Yes it will with that accent.
Tourist: Ha. Ha. Ha.
Me: Just kidding.
Tourist: Ok. It's also a two part question. First, where is the best Ice Cream place. Second, where is the best place to eat it?
Me: Well….that wasn't strange at all? (rolling eyes)
Tourist: Really?
Me: No. I've always wanted to be a life coach.
Tourist: Life Coach?
Me: You basically just asked me to guide you step by step on how and where to eat.
Tourist: Well, we really meant where is the best place to sit and watch birds.
Me: Actually, that would have made more sense.
Tourist: We thought it sounded silly.
Me: I think birds are silly, but the question would have been legitimate.
Tourist: Why do you think birds are silly?
Me: No reason. I just do.
Tourist: Oh.
Me: What kind of birds you wanting to see? Pelicans, Emu's, Seagulls?
Tourist: Obviously not here in the Mountains.
Me: That makes sense.
Tourist: We like Hummingbirds.
Me: Do you like Pigeons?
Tourist: No.
Me: Yeah, me either. They are literally in my top five most hated things on Earth.
Tourist: Why is that?
Me: Let's just say I've had one too many Pigeon attacks.
Tourist: Oh, sorry.
Me: It's ok.
Tourist: So, any suggestions?
Me: Sure. That park bench across the street. Ice Cream next door also. I'd say that's the best place for sure.
Tourist: Ok great!! Thanks!
Me: (smirking) No problem.

Ice Cream and Birds Continued....

20 Minutes Later:

Tourist: (Angry) Hey!!! You sent us to that park bench!
Me: I know. I'm the one who did it.
Tourist: We got bombarded by Pigeons!!
Me: Yeah, I kinda figured that would happen.
Tourist: Then why did you recommend it!? We got attacked!
Me: I just wanted you to share in my hatred for Pigeons. So, how was the Ice Cream?

#45 THE LIQUOR STORE

Tourist: Hey man, could you tell me where the nearest Liquor Store is?
Me: Well, there is one on either end of town. We are right in the middle.
Tourist: Which one is closer?
Me: We are exactly in between both of them.
Tourist: So which one is closer?
Me: I said exactly. In the middle. Of both of them.
Tourist: I understand.
Me: You do?
Tourist: Fine then. So which one is better?
Me: It depends on what you are looking for.
Tourist: (head down, shuffling feet) Well, you know.
Me: Ahhhhh….gotcha.
Tourist: So?
Me: I have no idea what you are talking about.
Tourist: I need the hard stuff.
Me: Oh, you mean frozen drinks?
Tourist: No. The hard liquor.
Me: That's what a frozen drink is.
Tourist: No, you're not understanding.
Me: Yes I am. You just aren't following.
Tourist: I want some of the higher alcohol stuff.
Me: Oh.
Tourist: Now you get it?
Me: I already had it.
Tourist: What?
Me: Nevermind. So, anyway, they both have what you need.
Tourist: So which one is closer?
Me: The one on the left.
Tourist: I thought you said we were exactly in the middle?
Me: You are kidding me right?
Tourist: No.
Me: Tell me the truth. You've already been to both.
Tourist: No.
Me: Yes you have.
Tourist: If I had, I wouldn't be asking you where they are.
Me: You're a tourist. You could be standing in line at the liquor store, bottle in hand, and ask the cashier where the liquor store is. I'm not stupid.

#46 PONCHOS

Tourist: (dripping wet) Excuse me Sir, do you know where we could buy some ponchos?
Me: I think you are too late.
Tourist: You sold out?
Me: (Oh geez) Ummmm…..no. I meant you are already soaked.
Tourist: Oh, yeah. We already knew that.
Me: At least that's a start I guess.
Tourist: Huh?
Me: So, you need ponchos right?
Tourist: Yes please.
Me: How many would you like?
Tourist: Two. How much are they?
Me: $5.
Tourist: Oh ok great! Here's $10.
Me: Don't forget about the tax. It's $11.18.
Tourist: Oh, whoops!!
Me: No problem.
Tourist: All I have is a $10 bill. Do you accept credit cards?
Me: Yes.
Tourist: Great!
Me: There is a small problem though.
Tourist: What's that?
Me: I don't sell ponchos.
Tourist: What???!!!
Me: Yeah. Matter of fact, I don't sell anything.
Tourist: But…
Me: (cutting her off) But nothing.
Tourist: So what do we do now?
Me: I'd recommend buying a towel.

SHORT AND STUPID

Tourist: (Frantic) Hey! Please Help! Have you seen my child!
Me: Oh my...boy or girl and what are they wearing?
Tourist: It's a boy and he's wearing a red t-shirt and blue shorts!
Me: Oh yeah. I see him. He's tugging on your back pocket.
Tourist: Oh (Speed Walks away)

#47 HIKING STICKS

Tourist: Howdy!
Me: Yo.
Tourist: Nice weather huh?
Me: If you like is sunny and beautiful then yes.
Tourist: I love it!
Me: Me too!
Tourist: So maybe you can help us. We are going hiking and need to find a place that has good hiking sticks.
Me: Oh yeah, I'm definitely your man on that topic!
Tourist: Great!
Me: Do you have your own saw?
Tourist: Huh?
Me: Saw. Like RRRRRRRRRRRRRRRRRR!!! Saw.
Tourist: Ummmm, no. Why would we need that?
Me: To make a hiking stick. Saw down a tree.
Tourist: Noooo. We meant a store that sells them.
Me: That's no fun.
Tourist: Well, we don't have time to do all of that.
Me: You got time to go walk on a trail for hours but you can't make a little stick?
Tourist: Seriously man, is there a place that sells them or not?
Me: I'm sure there is.
Tourist: Do you know where?
Me: I'm sure I don't.
Tourist: Well alright then. It's been nice talking to you I guess.
Me: Wait. I'm not done.
Tourist: Huh?
Me: I want to tell you a quick story.
Tourist: About what?
Me: The hiking stick accident of 1987.
Tourist: Seriously? A story about a hiking stick accident?
Me: No. Hahahahah! I'm just kidding. See you later.
Tourist: Ok then.
Me: Oh, by the way, if you want to buy a hiking stick, look for stores that have signs that say "Hiking Sticks."

#48 APPLE SAUCE

Tourist: Excuse me, do you know where I could get some Applesauce?
Me: (Oh my.. this is gonna be fun) Where's your baby?
Tourist: Huh?
Me: The applesauce is for a baby, right?
Tourist: Ummm...no, for me.
Me: Oh. Special diet?
Tourist: No. Just tell me where.
Me: What kind? Gala, green, sour, granny smith....
Tourist: (cutting me off) Just.....applesauce!
Me: I really like apples. I mean a lot.
Tourist: (Agitated yet confused) Well, I've only had regular applesauce. Are there different kinds?
Me: No.
Tourist: Then why did you ask about all those?
Me: Cuz you made me think of all the different kinds. I would have kept going but you cut me off.
Tourist: So where is best place? (noticeably angry)
Me: Secret barn.
Tourist: Have a name? (furious)
Me: (leaning in whispering) Secret. Barn.
Tourist: You are strange.
Me: No, sir, I'm just a man who likes apples and whispering.

#49 MY WIFE

Tourist: Hey!
Me: Hi, how are you!
Tourist: You're acting weird.
Me: No I'm not. Did you need help with something?
Tourist: Like what?
Me: Finding an attraction, bathroom, hiking trail, etc.
Tourist: Ummm…no….I'm your wife.
Me: You look like a tourist.
Tourist:(apparently my wife) No. I'm not a tourist. I'm your wife Jenny.
Me: That's a pretty name.
Tourist: This is ridiculous.
Me: Yes it is. You're right. This tourist role play is doing nothing for me.

#50 WHERE'S MY CAR?

Tourist: (frantic) Hey, have you seen my car?!
Me: (very calm and quiet) Yes.
Tourist: Well where is it?
Me: What's the make, model, and color?
Tourist: (screaming) What? I thought you have seen my car?!
Me: I'm sure I've seen your car. I mean, unless you drive some weird kind of car I've never seen before.
Tourist: What? Are you kidding me???!!!
Me: No. I've literally seen every kind of car before.
Tourist: (mad) My car was parked right there, now it's gone!
Me: This is exciting!
Tourist: What is exciting?
Me: I love mysteries and magic. Maybe a magician did it!
Tourist: That's ridiculous!
Me: Yeah. It could be a sinkhole!
Tourist: You have really made me mad! Who's your boss?
Me: I don't even know!
Tourist: I'm done here. (Walks away)
Me: (yelling) Hey, by the way, they towed your car. You parked at a stop light. Have a good one!

#51 AIRBRUSH T-SHIRT

Tourist: Hello! Maybe you could help me.
Me: I'm glad you said maybe. I'm a bit wishy washy when it comes to helping people.
Tourist: Haha. Ok. So, I want to buy an airbrush t-shirt, but I don't know what to get on it.
Me: Yeah, this should be fun. I'm very creative.
Tourist: Cool! I want one that really captures this town.
Me: Gotcha. So, first of all, you HAVE to put your name on it.
Tourist: Oh ok. Yeah, I wondered about that.
Me: (drawing on paper) So, what's your name?
Tourist: Lisa.
Me: Ok. Let's use the name Amanda.
Tourist: Huh?
Me: Identity theft. Gotta be smart around here.
Tourist: That doesn't make any sense.
Me: Sure it does. Say you're walking down the strip, someone sees your name on your t-shirt, then names their baby Lisa. That's identity theft.
Tourist: No, that's ridiculous.
Me: Well, I'm not going to be the one to lose my shirt, no pun intended.
Tourist: I think you are crazy. Just out of curiosity, what else you think I should put on it?
Me: I would seriously consider putting a picture of another Airbrush T-shirt on your Airbrush T-shirt.
Tourist: Ok, now that's the craziest idea I've ever heard. What sense would that make?
Me: Well, you said you wanted to capture what this town is really about. That would pretty much cover it.

#52 MULLET TRICKERY

Me: Hey you…over there! Come here!
Tourist: (walks over) Yes?
Me: I was wondering. Where did you get that top hat?
Tourist: At a Magic Shop.
Me: Really?
Tourist: Yep.
Me: Is there a rabbit in there?
Tourist: (laughing) No.
Me: So it's a worthless hat?
Tourist: No. It's pretty cool.
Me: What does it do?
Tourist: Sits on my head.
Me: Does it come with the mullet hanging out?
Tourist: Excuse me?
Me: I was just curious if the hair in the back was part of the hat, or if it was your own.
Tourist: It's my own hair.
Me: Oh, I thought it was some kind of mullet trickery.
Tourist: No, and I don't find that funny.
Me: I do.
Tourist: Whatever dude.
Me: I used to have a mullet, so I'm allowed to say that.
Tourist: Yeah whatever.
Me: Hey, speaking of that…do you know what the statute of limitations is for me being able to talk about mullets? I had mine back in the 80's when it was socially acceptable.
Tourist: What in the world are you talking about?
Me: I really don't know. Sometimes I just talk about random things.
Tourist: Well I'm done here.
Me: Ok fine. I'm going to go find this magic shop and get me a mullet hat.

Pancakes keep families together.

~No one ever said this~

~Matter of fact I didn't even type this~

#53 THE PUTT-PUTT GUY

Tourist: (Holding his own Putter) Hey. Which Putt Putt place is the best one?
Me: Did you steal that Putter?
Tourist: No, it's mine.
Me: Oh, that makes perfect sense.
Tourist: Do you know?
Me: Hey. Did you know you are carrying around a Putt Putt Putter? Haha, that's hard to say really fast.
Tourist: Huh?
Me: You say it. Like five times really fast. Putt Putt Putter.
Tourist: What are you talking about?
Me: Putt Putt Putter, Putt Putt Putter, Putt Putt Putter, Pu...
Tourist: (Cutting me off) I get it.
Me: I wish you would have said it. That would have been funny since you are holding it.
Tourist: (frustrated) So, I take it you don't know.
Me: I know all about Putt Putt. I've been playing it since I was like three.
Tourist: That's just great. So where is the best one?
Me: Indoor or Outdoor?
Tourist: Well, since it's snowing, I'll take indoor.
Me: Yeah, I'd recommend that. Don't want to wet your putter.
Tourist: So, best indoor one?
Me: Black light or just pitch black.
Tourist: There has to be light.
Me: No, it's more fun in pitch black. Balls everywhere, putters to the head.
Tourist: I'll take the black light.
Me: Ok. One last question. You want there to be Donkeys or Circus Clowns?
Tourist: What?
Me: I meant the Putt Putt theme, not your competition. I highly doubt Donkeys would be good at Putt Putt.
Tourist: I don't really care.
Me: Ok, that helps me narrow it down.
Tourist: So, what's your recommendation?
Me: Nothing. I narrowed it down to nothing.

#54 CORN DOGS

Tourist: I need a Corn Dog man. Where should I go?
Me: You sound like my kids.
Tourist: (leaning in mad) Excuse me?
Me: That's how my kids talk in the back seat. "I need a Corn Dog Dad."
Tourist: Yeah I'm not your kid.
Me: Obviously. You are too old.
Tourist: Whatever. I guess I'll get someone else to help me.
Me: No, No. I was just kidding. I can help you.
Tourist: I don't feel like wasting my time.
Me: Do you want to waste your time asking someone else who knows nothing about good Corn Dogs?
Tourist: Fine. Tell me.
Me: About why I know so much about Corn Dogs? It's a really long story. I will tell you though if you would like.
Tourist: No. I meant tell me where to get one.
Me: Are you sure you don't want to hear my story?
Tourist: Yes, I'm sure. I'm starving.
Me: Ok then. It's a really good story though.
Tourist: I'll pass.
Me: Ok. So, you want to know where to get a really good Corn Dog, correct?
Tourist: (Angry) Yes!!!!
Me: Can I ask you one question first, just to make sure I give you accurate information?
Tourist: Sure. What?
Me: What, exactly, is a Corn Dog?
Tourist: Are you freaking kidding me!?
Me: No.
Tourist: I thought you said you got your kids Corn Dogs all the time.
Me: No, I said they asked. I always tell them to shut up.

VACATION ITINERARY

1. Get lost on backroad.
2. Ask for directions.
3. Eat Pancakes.
4. After eating pancakes, ask someone where a Pancake place is.
5. Get T-Shirt with my name on it and picture of a Wolf.
6. Count Squirrels.
7. Wear first 3 items I pull out of suitcase or garbage bag.
8. Think of a dumb thought, then form a question using dumb thought, then ask that question to someone local.
9. Buy a Magnet for refrigerator.
10. Begin Refrigerator Magnet collection and ask for them at every store.
11. Pass 37 Pancake places then yell at kids in backseat to quit goofing off and keep eye open for Pancake place.
12. Lose car in parking lot.
13. Go on hike, but get distracted before hike by Putt Putt. After Putt Putt, convince self that I walked just as much as I would have hiked.
14. Buy lawn chair.
15. Sit in lawn chair on side of the road until a parade comes, even if it takes several weeks.
16. Chase pigeons on sidewalk.
17. Complain at hotel front desk that pool is too small. Then find out it was a Jacuzzi, not a pool.
18. Call relatives back home and have them wire money due to Refrigerator Magnet Collection getting out of hand.
19. Ask someone for directions to bathroom, but walk away while they are telling me.
20. Get bored with Refrigerator Magnet Collection, begin Ceramic Bear Collection.

#55 THE WOODEN SIGN

Tourist: Hey there.
Me: Why hello there.
Tourist: Let me ask you… Do you know where I could buy a wooden sign to hang outside my home?
Me: What you gonna have it say?
Tourist: Home.
Me: That's it?
Tourist: Yeah.
Me: Hmmm.
Tourist: What?
Me: Sounds boring.
Tourist: Well, it's not supposed to be exciting.
Me: Then why have it?
Tourist: To let people know it's my home.
Me: That is ridiculous.
Tourist: Why?
Me: People already know it's your home.
Tourist: Not everybody.
Me: Do you have a lot of random people just coming to your house?
Tourist: No, I live way out in the country.
Me: Do you have a lot of people come over? For like parties and stuff?
Tourist: No. Never.
Me: Can the animals near your house read?
Tourist: (Confused) Huh?
Me: Never mind. Can I give you a suggestion for your sign?
Tourist: Only if you can tell me where to get one.
Me: Sure.
Tourist: Fine.
Me: It should say "Halfway Home."
Tourist: What's that mean?
Me: Don't worry about it. Just put it up. Sign place is two miles that way.

#56 THE FISHERMAN

Tourist: How ya doin?
Me: Can't complain. Well, I take that back. I have a lot to complain about. Wanna hear?
Tourist: (laughing) Not really but thanks.
Me: You're welcome.
Tourist: Ok, so anyway, where is a good place to fish around here?
Me: What kind of fish? Bass? Trout? Shark?
Tourist: Definitely not Shark.
Me: I don't blame you. They are dangerous.
Tourist: There isn't an Ocean nearby anyway.
Me: Yes, I'm aware of that. I live here.
Tourist: Then why did you mention Shark?
Me: Because you weren't specific as to Geographic location.
Tourist: I thought the question was pretty obvious.
Me: I've learned not to ever assume.
Tourist: Ok fine. Let's say trout.
Me: Trout.
Tourist: No, let's say I want to fish for trout.
Me: I really, really want to say "I want to fish for trout", but I won't. I would sound like a seven year old mocking you.
Tourist: (agitated) Ok so I guess you aren't going to help me.
Me: Sounds fishy.
Tourist: Excuse me?
Me: I dunno. Just talking out loud.
Tourist: I see. Ok, thanks.
Me: Again, you're welcome. Glad to be of service.

#57 LIGHTNING AND JELLYFISH

Me: Hey you! Come here!
Tourist: Yes?
Me: You know it's lightning pretty serious out there and you are holding a metal hiking stick.
Tourist: And?
Me: You are making me nervous. You are too close to me.
Tourist: What are you worried about?
Me: I'm scared of lightning.
Tourist: Why?
Me: Because I want to be.
Tourist: What does that even mean?
Me: I don't know. I'm also scared of Jellyfish.
Tourist: Oooooo K then.
Me: My worst nightmare is to be hit by lightning while petting a Jellyfish. It would be like double electricity.
Tourist: That may be the dumbest thing I've ever heard.
Me: I might agree with you.
Tourist: So, I'm just going to go stand over here some more.
Me: You shouldn't.
Tourist: Because of the lightning?
Me: No.
Tourist: What, Jellyfish going to fall out of the sky?
Me: Don't say that. That's horrible.
Tourist: You are weird my friend.
Me: Ok fine. Can I give you one little piece of advice though?
Tourist: About the lightning again?
Me: No. About not standing there.
Tourist: Standing where? On the sidewalk?
Me: Ummmm, no. You are not on the sidewalk. You are standing in the middle of a Trolley stop, and there is one right behind you.
Tourist: (jumping) Oh crap!!!

SHORT AND STUPID

Tourist: Hi.
Me: Hello.
Tourist: (Got distracted by someone honking and left)

#58 RELEASE THE BEARS

Tourist: Hey man.
Me: Hey.
Tourist: Do you know what time they release the Bears?
Me: (clearing throat) Did you say Release the Bears?
Tourist: Yup. What time they let em' go?
Me: From where?
Tourist: Don't they keep em' in cages?
Me: Are you being serious? I need to know before I tell you.
Tourist: Man I'm dead serious. I know they can't just let them all run loose all the time. That would be too dangerous. Too many people here.
Me: Ok. I'm going to pretend you are being serious and answer you.
Tourist: (totally oblivious) Cool.
Me: They usually let em' go around noon.
Tourist: Do they feed them before they let them go? I've heard they rummage through garbage cans.
Me: Oh sure. But they sometimes want to eat more.
Tourist: Oh. I guess cuz they are Bears.
Me: Yeah, I guess.
Tourist: Do they ever come into town?
Me: Depends on what's going on.
Tourist: Like what?
Me: They usually come for Chili cook-offs. Rib Fest. Things like that.
Tourist: Oh I bet they do!
Me: Y…..up.
Tourist: Well man I was just curious.
Me: Will you do me a favor?
Tourist: Sure man.
Me: If you see a Bear in town at night, let me know.
Tourist: Ok but why.
Me: Because they have a curfew and I'll need to let the authorities know.
Tourist: Sure thing man.
Me: Thanks. It's good to know there are smart, responsible people like you out there looking out for other people.
Tourist: I try man, I try.
Me: Well, I better go. I'm going to go write a book about tourists.
Tourist: Later.

#59 FLOWERS AND SHORTY SHORTS

Tourist: (Woman wearing close to nothing... very short shorts and see through shirt)Hey, are you allowed to pick flowers in the Mountains?
Me: Who me? No, I'm not allowed to.
Tourist: No, I meant in general.
Me: I'm not really sure if I'm allowed to pick flowers in any Mountains.
Tourist: No. I mean can anybody pick flowers inside the Park?
Me: Probably scientists.
Tourist: But not me?
Me: I'm not in charge. I'd hate to give you false permission.
Tourist: No, I don't think you are understanding what I'm asking. Is it legal for someone to pick flowers and take them out of the park?
Me: No, it's not legal.
Tourist: Ok. Whew. That's all I was wanting to know.
Me: You also can't pick up animals and take them out of the park.
Tourist: Yeah, I figured that.
Me: You also can't pick up rocks and take them out of the park.
Tourist: Ok yeah.
Me: You also can't run naked in the park.
Tourist: What?
Me: Naked means no clothes.
Tourist: I know that but why are you telling me that?
Me: I'm trying to cover all the bases. And your body parts.
Tourist: Yeah, I just wanted to know about flowers.
Me: I like flowers.
Tourist: That's nice.
Me: I was just kidding. I'm a dude. I don't really care.
Tourist: Ok. I'm going to leave.
Me: Ok. Keep your clothes on this time please.

#60 SPEAKING OF SHORTY SHORTS

Me: Excuse me! Excuse me ma'am! You dropped something!
Tourist: Oh! What did I drop?
Me: The rest of your pants!
Tourist: Huh?
Me: All I can see is your pockets! I think the rest fell off somewhere!
Tourist: No, they are supposed to be that way!
Me: Really?
Tourist: Yeah. It's the new style.
Me: Really?
Tourist: Yep.
Me and Tourist: (Long, awkward silence)
Me: Ok. So, the objective is for people to see what's in your pockets?
Tourist: No. It's just fashion.
Me: What type of fashion?
Tourist: I dunno.
Me: Me either.
Tourist: Well, I guess I'll go now.
Me: Ok. I really don't know what to say.
Tourist: About what?
Me: Anything.
Tourist: Me either.
Me: I figured.
Tourist: Figured what.
Me: You probably didn't have anything to say.
Tourist: Oh.
Me: Yeah.
Tourist: Ok.
Me: Bye.
Tourist: Bye.
Me: (To myself) What just happened?

#61 WATCH MY KID FOR ME

Tourist: I have a strange request.
Me: I like strange requests.
Tourist: Good!
Me: So what do you need?
Tourist: Is there any way possible that you could watch our son for about half an hour?
Me: Huh?
Tourist: We want to go into that Adult store across the street. We don't want to take him in there and you look pretty dependable.
Me: Seriously?
Tourist: Yes.
Me: So "pretty" dependable is good enough for you?
Tourist: Ummm yeah. We will just be across the street.
Me: What if I told you I was probably below average dependable.
Tourist: What?
Me: I'm just kidding. I'm actually great with kids. I have four boys myself!
Tourist: Great! So you will do it!
Me: No. Go away. You are nuts.

Them stupid Go-Karts got my Wedding Dress dirty.

~Ugh~

#62 THE BOBCAT…MAYBE

Tourist #1: Hey man. Maybe you can solve a dispute my buddy and I are having.
Me: Sure! I love disputes! If I don't solve it are you guys gonna punch each other?
Tourist #1: Huh?
Me: I was kind of just kidding.
Tourist #1: Oh hahahaha.
Me: So what's the dispute?
Tourist #2: (yelling) He said we saw a Bobcat in the Mountains but I think it was a Fox.
Me: Ooooooooooooo K.
Tourist #1: Dude it was a Bobcat!
Tourist #2: It was not!
Me: Was it a Cat at all?
Tourist #1: Is a Bobcat really a cat? I thought it was more like a Wolf.
Me: Yeah no.
Tourist #2: See man it was a Fox!
Me: I thought he said it was like a Wolf.
Tourist #1: It was.
Tourist #2: Then what does a Fox look like?
Me: I think you guys saw a Dog.
Tourist #1: No way. It was black and fuzzy.
Me: Ok. That eliminates Bobcat, Fox, and probably Wolf.
Tourist #2: Then what could it be?

THE BOBCAT...MAYBE CONTINUED...

Me: Was it big?
Tourist #1: No, very small.
Me: Did you guys eat any of the Mushrooms in the Mountains?
Tourist #2: No way dude. We aren't that stupid.
Me: Yeah, you are right. Matter of fact, I think it was probably a Bobcat. You should both go home and describe exactly what you saw to all your friends and tell them you confirmed it as a Bobcat.
Both Tourists Simultaneously: Sweet dude!!! Thanks!

#63 HOT AIR BALLOONS

Tourist: Hey, what's up with all the Hot Air Balloons?
Me: Ummmm....there aren't any Hot Air Balloons.
Tourist: Are you sure?
Me: Yes. Very.
Tourist: Hmmm. Come to think of it I haven't actually seen one either. That's strange. (walks away shaking head)
Me: (Crying)

#64 LONG AND STUPID

Tourist: Hey.
Me: Hey.
Tourist: How are you this evening?
Me: I'm super duper great. You?
Tourist: Awesome.
Me: So what can I do for you?
Tourist: Oh, nothing. Just walking around talking to people.
Me: That's a good idea. You can learn a lot from the locals.
Tourist: Anything interesting going on with you?
Me: Are you hitting on me?
Tourist: No man.
Me: Oh ok. Just checking.
Tourist: No I'm just bored.
Me: Yeah me too. We should get a burger.
Tourist: Huh?
Me: I'm hungry.
Tourist: Oh.
Me: So what have you learned from other locals?
Tourist: To be careful at crosswalks for one. They said I could get hit by a car.
Me: Who told you that? That's ridiculous!
Tourist: What do you mean?
Me: You don't need to be careful! Just go!
Tourist: Really?
Me: Yeah. Even if they hit you, it's their fault.
Tourist: O....k.
Me: So what else?
Tourist: Don't feed the Bears.
Me: Again, nonsense.
Tourist: Well they said it was a bad idea.
Me: Nope. Good idea.
Tourist: Why?
Me: If it bites or eats you, again…not your fault.
Tourist: That's just stupid.

Long And Stupid....Continued

Me: Well, it rarely happens.
Tourist: I don't want to take the chance.
Me: I'd like for you to take the chance.
Tourist: Oh really?
Me: Yeah. You seem like you need a little excitement.
Tourist: I guess.
Me: (laughing so hard on the inside) Yeah. I can hook you up.
Tourist: Suggestions?
Me: Yeah. Zipline without a harness.
Tourist: Now that's stupid!
Me: Putt Putt without a putter.
Tourist: Ok that wouldn't make sense.
Me: Bungee jump....no cord.
Tourist: These ideas are terrible.
Me: I can keep going.
Tourist: No, that's ok. Unless you actually have a GOOD suggestion.
Me: I rarely have good suggestions nor do I make good decisions.
Tourist: Well that's not smart!
Me: But I graduated College.
Tourist: I don't know how!
Me: Yeah, me either. So what are you doing next?
Tourist: Renting a Scooter I think. Going to ride through the Mountains.
Me: Don't wear a helmet.
Tourist: Yeah, see you later.
Me: Maybe. Depends on whether or not you wear the helmet.

#65 WHY IS IT SO DARK?

Tourist: Hey you. Why is it so dark outside?
Me: Hold on. Let me get prepared for this.
Tourist: Huh?
Me: Ok, I'm mentally ready. Now what did you ask?
Tourist: Why it's so dark.
Me: Oh, yeah, that's right. Ummm, there is no sun.
Tourist: Yeah I noticed.
Me: That pretty much sums it up.
Tourist: Why ain't there more lights?
Me: Because they don't need any more lights.
Tourist: Yes they do. It's really dark.
Me: It's called night time.
Tourist: Don't be funny with me.
Me: I'm not. I could be though.
Tourist: Whatever. So you have no idea why they don't have more lights here?
Me: Yeah, I have an idea.
Tourist: And?
Me: I don't like to share my ideas. Someone might steal them.
Tourist: That's just dumb.
Me: You are the one wondering why it's so dark. Not me.
Tourist: Yeah whatever. (starts to walk away)
Me: Hey, be careful. It's dark out there.
Tourist: (comes back angry) Are you making fun of me?
Me: No. I said "Be careful, there's a shark out there."
Tourist: Yeah right.
Me: Even if there was a shark out there, you wouldn't know it.
Tourist: How's that?
Me: Because it's too dark.

#66 SOME GUY NAMED JIMMY

Tourist: Hey, have you seen Jimmy?
Me: Is it in theaters?
Tourist: No man. My friend Jimmy.
Me: Ok. So, I'm assuming I know him and you know me?
Tourist: No. We are from Texas.
Me: Ok. So, you want to know where Jimmy from Texas is, right?
Tourist: Pretty much.
Me: I have no idea.
Tourist: So you haven't seen him.
Me: No. Wait a second.....no.
Tourist: Are you sure?
Me: Is he wearing an Airbrush T-Shirt or something that says Jimmy from Texas on it?
Tourist: No.
Me: Is he a Giant?
Tourist: (surprised) No dude!
Me: Is his name Chris?
Tourist: No, it's Jimmy. I already told you.
Me: Have you been drinking?
Tourist: Yes.
Me: Has Jimmy been drinking?
Tourist: Yeah. A lot.
Me: Ok. So, let me get this straight. I'm supposed to help two drunk guys from Texas find each other in one of the most populated tourist destinations in America?
Tourist: Yup.
Me: And I don't know what one of them looks like?
Tourist: I don't know how you don't know Jimmy.
Me: Is your name Jimmy?
Tourist: No.
Me: He's across the street. Run fast and don't look both ways

#67 NOT GOOD WITH NUMBERS

Me: Hey you! Come here!
Tourist: Yeah what you want?
Me: I have a question. I see so many pretty southern girls with really, really ugly guys.
Tourist: So?
Me: For example, you are like a 9 and your husband is like a 4.
Tourist: So?
Me: I'm just curious. How does that happen?
Tourist: Oh. That's simple. I can't count good.

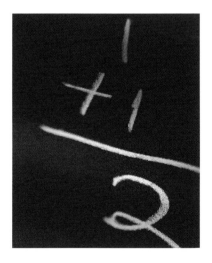

I collect Ceramic Bears so my Grandkids will have something special someday.

~Why did I put that in this book~

#68 CERAMIC BEARS

Tourist: Hi, how are you Sir?
Me: I'm great. And you?
Tourist: I'm great! I wonder if you could help me?
Me: I'll try my best.
Tourist: Ok. I collect Ceramic Bears, and I'm looking for one in particular.
Me: Oh. I see. Haha, do I look like someone who collects them too?
Tourist: No, I just thought you could help.
Me: Well, I actually do.
Tourist: (Insanely Surprised) Really?!
Me: Of course. We all do around here.
Tourist: I didn't realize that! Everyone else I've asked doesn't know what I'm talking about.
Me: Well, they are just being secretive. You know how crazy Ceramic Bear collectors can be.
Tourist: No, actually I don't.
Me: Oh. I've seen things that would make you cry.
Tourist: Like what?
Me: Once, I saw two women fighting over a Ceramic Bear playing a Fiddle under a Waterfall. It fell and broke.
Tourist: What happened?
Me: They screamed and yelled about it being the last one. Finally, they just walked away.
Tourist: That's awful! I've never seen that one.
Me: You probably never will. It was special I tell you.

CERAMIC BEARS CONTINUED.....

Tourist: Sounds like it.
Me: So, which one are you looking for?
Tourist: Oh, it's a Blue Bear smiling.
Me: I've never seen it. Heard rumors, but never seen it.
Tourist: Really? What have you heard?
Me: That's it's extremely rare.
Tourist: Oh. Really? Because I looked it up and it only sells for around $6.99.
Me: Are you sure it wasn't $6,999.00?
Tourist: Yeah, I'm sure.
Me: Hmmm. I would check all the Candy Stores.
Tourist: Huh?
Me: Yeah. Candy Stores.
Tourist: Why?
Me: Look...have you been able to find one yet?
Tourist: No.
Me: Have you checked all the other places that carry them?
Tourist: Yes.
Me: Then try Candy Stores.
Tourist: That doesn't make sense.
Me: You are searching for a Blue Ceramic Bear that's smiling.
Tourist: And?
Me: Exactly.

#69 THE GUY WHO REFUSED TO BELIEVE WHERE HE WAS

Tourist: Hey man, I need some serious help.
Me: Have you been injured?
Tourist: No.
Me: Good. I'm not qualified for that.
Tourist: Oh. So I don't know where I'm at.
Me: Are you sure you don't have a head injury?
Tourist: Yeah, I'm sure. I mean what town is this?
Me: Gatlinburg.
Tourist: No, it's not.
Me: Yeah, it is.
Tourist: What state?
Me: Tennessee.
Tourist: There's no way. Not possible.
Me: Well, it is.
Tourist: There is no way I'm in Tennessee, and this doesn't look like Gatlinburg.
Me: Where are you from?
Tourist: Minnesota.
Me: Have you been to Gatlinburg before?
Tourist: No. Never.
Me: Have you been to Tennessee before?
Tourist: Nope.
Me: So, how do you know this isn't Gatlinburg if you've never been here?
Tourist: I've seen pictures.
Me: Were they black and white pictures from 1920?
Tourist: No.
Me: Well, I think I know what is going on now.
Tourist: What do you mean?
Me: You're right, this isn't Gatlinburg, TN.
Tourist: I knew it! Where am I?
Me: The Bahamas.
Tourist: I know that's not right.
Me: Sir, I'm pretty sure you don't.

#70 I'M BEING FOLLOWED

Tourist: (Out of breath) Hey, please help me!
Me: What's the problem?
Tourist: I'm being followed.
Me: By who?
Tourist: I don't know. He started way back but is getting closer. I start walking fast or jogging and he does too.
Me: That's strange. Especially in the broad daylight.
Tourist: I know. And I can't find my husband. I went into a store and came out and he was gone.
Me: That's not good. Did you call his Cellphone?
Tourist: Yeah, but it's dead.
Me: Hmmm. Well, why don't you just wait here and we'll see if he catches up. Just to be safe.
Tourist: Ok thank you so much!
Me: No problem.

A FEW MINUTES LATER…….

Tourist: Here he comes.
Me: Ok. I'm watching.
Tourist: Uh oh. Now I feel stupid.
Me: Why?
Tourist: It was my husband following me.
Me: Huh?
Tourist: Yeah. He is really slow. I guess I kept running and he kept chasing.
Me: Wow.
Tourist: I feel so stupid.
Me: Well, just be thankful. He should have gone the other way but didn't.

#71 TUBING

Tourist: Hi! Maybe you can point me in the right direction.
Me: That way.
Tourist: No. I meant help find somewhere.
Me: That's very vague but I will try.
Tourist: I haven't told you where yet.
Me: Oh.
Tourist: Anyway, where is the best and closest place to go Tubing?
Me: Water or no water?
Tourist: Ummmm, water of course.
Me: Ok. Some people don't like to get wet.
Tourist: What would be the point of that?
Me: To stay dry.
Tourist: (visibly frustrated) Ok, so where is best place to go River Tubing.
Me: Can you swim?
Tourist: Yes.
Me: That helps.
Tourist: What would that matter?
Me: If you couldn't swim I was going to send you to a creek.
Tourist: That's just ridiculous.
Me: I know.
Tourist: So, one last time, do you know?
Me: Yes.
Tourist: And?
Me: Sorry, I meant to say no.
Tourist: Why are you doing this?
Me: Doing what?
Tourist: Being frustrating.
Me: Oh. Because the tubing places are closed. It's January and freezing.
Tourist: Oh. Ok. Bye.

#72 I THINK WE'RE GOING TO GET MARRIED

Me: (Yelling) Hey guys! Congratulations!

Tourist: Huh?

Me: You are wearing a Wedding Dress and A Tux!

Tourist: So?

Me: Did you just get married? Or are you about to?

Tourist: We are thinking about it.

Me: What????!!!!!

Tourist: We can't decide.

Me: On where?

Tourist: No. Whether or not we want to be married.

Me: Do you know each other?

Tourist: Yes.

Me: That's good enough. Do it.

Tourist: It's more complicated than that.

Me: No it's not.

Tourist: Ok then. I guess we will see you later.

Me: I'll throw rice if you walk back by. Or blow bubbles.

Tourist: Why?

Me: Ummm….Do you guys have any clue what's going on?

Tourist: Not really.

Me: Ok. Well, you guys are perfect for each other. Dangerous to society, but perfect for each other. See ya.

#73 WHY IS IT SO HOT HERE?

Tourist: Hey, why is it so hot here?
Me: Because the Sun is out and it's Summer.
Tourist: Is it always this hot?
Me: Yes. Year round. Every day, every hour.
Tourist: I bet you get tired of that heat then.
Me: Are you guys from around here or Earth?
Tourist: Yeah about an hour away.
Me: Seriously?
Tourist: Yeah.
Me: Do you live underground?
Tourist: What?
Me: How is it you guys live only an hour away and yet think this is like a tropical jungle.
Tourist: We didn't know.
Me: How did you get here?
Tourist: We drove.
Me: You shouldn't do that anymore.
Tourist: Do what?
Me: Leave where you came from.

SHORT AND STUPID

Tourist: Why don't you see any Bears down here?
Me: Huh?
Tourist: Been here a whole week and not seen a Bear.
Me: You mean in town?
Tourist: Yup.
Me: They can't stand to be around tourists.
Tourist: Why?
Me: Because they are extremely intelligent animals.

#74 THE KID TOURIST

Kid Tourist: Hi Mister.
Me: Hey! How are you?
Kid Tourist: I don't know.
Me: Me too!
Kid Tourist: (giggling)That's funny.
Me: Where are you from?
Kid Tourist: What?
Me: Where are you from?
Kid Tourist: What?
Me: Where are your Mom and Dad?
Kid Tourist: What?
Me: WHERE…..ARE…..YOUR….MOM AND DAD!?
Kid Tourist: Sitting on that bench.
Me: Oh, ok. What are you doing?
Kid Tourist: Talking to you.
Me: Is this the funnest thing you've done since you've been here?
Kid Tourist: No.
Me: Yeah, me either.
Kid Tourist: I saw some Jelly Beans.
Me: Wow that's super exciting.
Kid Tourist: They were blue.
Me: Well Ok. Tell your Mom and Dad to come get you.
Kid Tourist: What?
Me: (yelling) Come get your little boy! He's all hopped up on Blue Jelly Beans and talking nonsense!

#75 THE REALLY DRUNK GUY

Tourist: (stumbling towards me) Hey…hey…hey man.
Me: (Having a huge Mental Party in my head) What's up dude?
Tourist: Hey….hey….hey…..
Me: Exactly.
Tourist: Hey man. Hey. Hey you got anything to drink?
Me: Water.
Tourist: No man hey no. Like you know alcohol hey man.
Me: No. I don't want to end up like you.
Tourist: Hey man that's not cool. Hey, what are you talking about?
Me: I don't want to stumble around town saying "hey" over and over.
Tourist: Hey man hey hey hey….man. I ain't doing that.
Me: Hey whatever.
Tourist: Hey man you just said hey.
Me: What have you been doing?
Tourist: (slurring and stumbling backwards) Don't you wanna know?!!
Me: I could guess, but no, I don't really care.
Tourist: Hey man I come here all the time.
Me: Yeah, I know.
Tourist: Hey man I ain't no tourist man. You know hey.
Me: You are what I call a local tourist.
Tourist: Hey man that doesn't make any sense.
Me: Yes it does. You are local but have no idea where anything is, why you are here, or what you are doing. Ever.
Tourist: Hey man. Ok. See ya.
Me: Great. I'll see you tomorrow. Same conversation as always.
Tourist: Hey man you got anything to drink?

#76 THE LEAVES ARE CHANGING

Tourist: Hi! Could you tell me about the leaves?
Me: Sure! They are on trees. What else?
Tourist: Haha! No, I meant when do they change colors?
Me: October, November.
Tourist: No. I meant when?
Me: I know. That's why I said October, November.
Tourist: No. I mean what time of day do they change colors?
Me: Huh?
Tourist: Well, I've noticed during the day they are very colorful, like Reds and yellows and stuff. But at night they seem like a darker green color.
Me: Where are you looking at them from?
Tourist: Our balcony. They are far away.
Me: You realize that it's because it's dark outside at night, right?
Tourist: No. What do you mean?
Me: I mean at night they all look dark. Everything does.
Tourist: Oh.
Me: Yup.
Tourist: So, they don't really change colors throughout the day?
Me: Are you from a desert?
Tourist: No.
Me: Have you ever been outside?
Tourist: Of course.
Me: You've never seen leaves change colors?
Tourist: No. It's too dark to see that happen.
Me: 8:52 p.m.
Tourist: Huh?
Me: That's what time they change colors each day. Bye Bye.

#77 POTATO GUN

Tourist: Hey you, do you know where I could find a Potato Gun?
Me: What???!!!
Tourist: Potato Gun.
Me: I heard you. Then I said "What???!!!
Tourist: So do you know?
Me: First, let me ask you why you need it.
Tourist: What's it matter?
Me: You didn't let me ask you yet.
Tourist: Fine. Ask.
Me: Why do you need it?
Tourist: It's none of your business.
Me: Well, I don't want to be responsible for some tourist walking around shooting people with potatoes.
Tourist: We aren't going to do that.
Me: How do I know that?
Tourist: Because we told you.
Me: Yeah, I don't believe you. You look like the type of person to shoot potatoes at people.
Tourist: What? Are you kidding me?
Me: No. However, I will say, you look more like a Mashed Potato shooter. You seem to have a softer side.
Tourist: This is the craziest conversation I've had in a while.
Me: Not for me.
Tourist: I can imagine.
Me: So, do you want to know where you can get a Mashed Potato Gun?
Tourist: Ummm…no. Just forget it.
Me: I'm glad I talked you out of it. That would have been messy.
Tourist: I'm sure it would.
Me: See. I knew you would finally admit to your plan.

#78 CAMPFIRE

Tourist: Hi.
Me: Don't even ask.
Tourist: Huh?
Me: Are you going to ask me about Bears?
Tourist: Oh…no, nothing like that.
Me: Whew….Ok, what do you need?
Tourist: We were just wondering if you are allowed to build a campfire close to town?
Me: How close?
Tourist: On our hotel porch balcony. We have our fire pit in the camper.
Me: Are you serious?
Tourist: About what?
Me: Anything you just said.
Tourist: Yes. We always take our fire pit on vacation. It's one of those small round metal ones. It comes in handy!
Me: I'm sure it does. So, you want to build a fire on your hotel balcony?
Tourist: Yes!!
Me: Don't you think you should ask the hotel people first?
Tourist: Oh, we already did. They said no way.
Me: Gotcha. So, you want me to give you permission?
Tourist: No, not permission. Just tell us if you think they are wrong.
Me: Of course they are wrong.
Tourist: Really? We've asked ten other people and they agreed with the hotel.
Me: Not me. I'm all for fires.
Tourist: Exactly!
Me: I have a feeling you guys are burning some special stuff in your fire!
Tourist: Yep! Marshmallows usually!
Me: Wow. Ok. Well, it was nice talking to you. I need to run. I'll be watching for you guys on the news!
Tourist: (confused) Ummm, Ok. See you later!

The thought of a Spider biting my leg makes me nervous. That's why I wear Knee High socks when I feed Bears out in the wild.

~I'm sure someone said this but we'll never know~

#79 SUNGLASSES

Me: (Yelling at some tourists who are being obnoxious) Hey!!!
Tourist: What?!
Me: Have you seen my sunglasses?
Tourist: Huh?
Me: Sunglasses.
Tourist: What are you talking about?
Me: Sunglasses.
Tourist: Yeah, heard that part dude. Why you asking us?
Me: Because I can't find them, and you are standing in front of me. Nobody else to ask.
Tourist: You think we took them?
Me: I didn't say that. But did you?
Tourist: How would we do that? We haven't even been near you.
Me: Maybe you are a Magician.
Tourist: That's just stupid dude.
Me: So.
Tourist: Yeah well good luck finding your sunglasses.
Me: I didn't lose my sunglasses.
Tourist: Huh?
Me: Oh are we playing stupid again?
Tourist: Excuse me?
Me: I said I didn't lose my sunglasses and that you are stupid.
Tourist: Are you looking for trouble?
Me: No, I'm looking for my sunglasses.
Tourist: (angry) Huh?
Me: There you go again being stupid.
Tourist: (so confused, he just turned and walked away shaking his head)
Me: (Yelling) Hey! I found my sunglasses! They are on my head! Thanks for the help stupid!

#80 BEARS ARE SCARY

Tourist: Hi, do you know a lot about Bears?
Me: Why yes I do.
Tourist: Great! So, are they scary up close?
Me: Ummm…yep.
Tourist: That's what I figured.
Me: Why are you asking?
Tourist: My wife wants to get close to pet one, but I told her it's not a good idea.
Me: Is she talking about real Bears? Or stuffed ones?
Tourist: Real Bears.
Me: Does she watch TV?
Tourist: Yes. That's why she wants to pet one.
Me: Oh. Well that's odd.
Tourist: Yeah, I know.
Me: Do you like your wife?
Tourist: Of course! What kind of question was that?!
Me: I was trying to figure out whether or not to tell you to tell her to pet one.
Tourist: Oh, hahaha.
Me: I was serious. Like her, no pet. Don't like her, give it a hug.
Tourist: That's just wrong.
Me: Well, she's the one wanting to pet a wild Bear. Not me.
Tourist: True.
Me: Do you want my honest advice?
Tourist: Yes!
Me: Ok. Find a really big dog, preferably a black one. Tell her it's a Bear.
Tourist: What? She will know the difference!
Me: Sir, are you really sure about that?

#81 BIG SNAKES

Tourist: Wow! We just saw a huge snake in the mountains!
Me: What kind was it?
Tourist: Huge!
Me: I know, but what kind?
Tourist: It was really big!
Me: Yeah, got that part. What color was it?
Tourist: Snake colors.
Me: Huh?
Tourist: Same color as all the snakes.
Me: Are you guys from outer space?
Tourist: What?
Me: I was just wondering what kind of snake you might have seen.
Tourist: It was a big one!!!
Me: How many legs did it have?
Tourist: Not sure. We couldn't see any.
Me: Ok. I think I know now what it was.
Tourist: What? We want to be able to tell our friends when we get home.
Me: Ok. I'm going to tell you what kind it was, but it's complicated. You might want to write it down so you can explain it to your friends.
Tourist: Sure! Can I borrow a pen?
Me: Yup. Ok, you ready?
Tourist: Yeah, go ahead.
Me: Huge. Snake. With colors.
Tourist: That's what we saw!
Me: Amazing.

#82 THE MASSAGE PARLOR

Tourist: Excuse me, do you know where a Massage Parlor is?
Me: Legal or illegal.
Tourist: What?
Me: Do you want an actual Massage Parlor or one of those "other" ones.
Tourist: An actual Massage Parlor.
Me: Then I don't know.
Tourist: So, you know about illegal ones then?
Me: Shhhhh.
Tourist: What?
Me: Don't say that out loud.
Tourist: Say what?
Me: Illegal stuff. My wife is here.
Tourist: Ohhhh. (whispering) So you know about illegal Massage Parlors?
Me: Yes.
Tourist: Well, maybe that will help my back.
Me: I'm sure it will.
Tourist: Where is it?
Me: Where is what?
Tourist: (still whispering) The illegal Massage Parlor.
Me: Speak up. I can't hear you.
Tourist: (still whispering) The illegal Massage Parlor.
Me: Seriously, it's Ok now. Just say it out loud.
Tourist: The illegal Massage Parlor!
Me: That's creepy.
Tourist: You told me to say it.
Me: You do realize that you are a tourist asking some random guy in a booth about an illegal Massage Parlor, right?
Tourist: Oh, yeah, you're right. Sorry to bother you.
Me: It's Ok. (whispering) By the way, I only charge $10.

#83 CANDY APPLES

Tourist: Who around here has the best Candy Apples?
Me: You talking to me?
Tourist: Yeah.
Me: Do I look like a Candy Apple expert?
Tourist: No. I just figured you knew.
Me: Well, I do.
Tourist: Yes!
Me: But I'm not allowed to tell anyone.
Tourist: Huh? Why not?
Me: It's a secret Candy Apple place.
Tourist: Ummmm... I would think they want the business.
Me: They don't.
Tourist: That doesn't make sense.
Me: Sure it does.
Tourist: No, it doesn't. Not at all.
Me: Yes, it does. They only make one a day. Then they eat it.
Tourist: What? That's crazy!
Me: I know! But it's the truth.
Tourist: Where is this place?
Me: I already told you. It's secret.
Tourist: You are making this up.
Me: I know.
Tourist: What a waste of my time.
Me: If you want, I can get you the secret Candy Apple they make.
Tourist: You already told me you made it all up.
Me: Oh yeah.
Tourist: Last time I'm asking. Is there a good place to get Candy Apples around here?
Me: Yes, but it's a secret.
Tourist: (furious) Same story as before?
Me: Of course not. I never make up the same story twice.

#84 TAKE MY PICTURE PLEASE

Tourist: Hey, could you take my picture?
Me: I would, but my camera is full.
Tourist: No, with my camera!
Me: Ohhhh… sure.
Tourist: Great! Thanks! Here you go.
Me: Oh, nice! Ok, I'm going to hit the button.
Tourist: I'm not ready.
Me: So this is a photo shoot?
Tourist: No, I just need a nice picture to send home.
Me: Oh.
Tourist: You can take more than one.
Me: It's Ok. I'll just take the one.
Tourist: I don't mind at all. I could use some nice pictures!
Me: I'm terrible at taking pictures.
Tourist: You can't be that bad.
Me: I am. One time a tourist asked me to take their picture and I threw their camera across the street.
Tourist: Oh, really? Well, that has nothing to do with taking bad pictures.
Me: Another time a tourist asked me to take a picture, and I dropped the camera and smashed it.
Tourist: (obviously nervous) Ohhhh… well, you know what, don't worry about it. I don't need a picture.
Me: No, it's fine. I promise. That was a long time ago when tourists frustrated me. I'm totally cool with it now.
Tourist: When was the last incident?
Me: Like an hour ago.
Tourist: Alright then. Just give me my camera.
Me: Fine. I was going to shoot something special!
Tourist: It's fine. I really don't need anything.
Me: Ok then. By the way, I took like seven pictures of my shoe with your camera. See ya.

#85 THE TOURIST OF ALL TOURISTS

(Guy Was Extremely Weird Before He Even Spoke)

Tourist: Hi, I need some serious help. Are you a tour guide or information center? I have quite a few questions about the area.
Me: I am now.
Tourist: What?
Me: Yes, I am. What can I help you with?
Tourist: Ok. First of all, I see a lot of attractions around here.
Me: Yes?
Tourist: That has nothing to do with my question.
Me: Huh? You were just telling me you see a lot of attractions around here?
Tourist: Sorry. I talk to myself out loud sometimes.
Me: Oh.
Tourist: Yeah. So, anyway, the Mountains.
Me: Yes?
Tourist: Are they cold?
Me: Huh? Like now?
Tourist: Yes.
Me: It's 27 degrees out.
Tourist: I know, but I thought it might be warmer up there.
Me: Sure it is. I'd go sleeveless for sure if you go.
Tourist: Hmmm, Ok. (writing that down)
Me: Anything else?
Tourist: Yes. If I go up there, what kind of animals should I expect to see?
Me: Are you wanting to find them, or not wanting to find them?
Tourist: Not wanting to find them.
Me: Giraffes. You won't find them.
Tourist: Giraffes?
Me: I said Lizard.
Tourist: Huh?
Me: Donkey.

THE TOURIST OF ALL TOURISTS CONTINUED.....

Tourist: Are you Ok?
Me: Yep!
Tourist: Why do you keep naming those animals?
Me: Well, I said Giraffes to be funny. Then I thought Lizards sounded funny. And everyone knows I love to say Donkey.
Tourist: I really wish you wouldn't mess around. I need to know these things for safety.
Me: Penguins.
Tourist: There aren't any Penguins here.
Me: I know.
Tourist: Then why did you say it?
Me: Seriously? Are you asking me this again? I'm just going to keep naming stupid animals until you catch on.
Tourist: Fine. Forget the animals. Next question. What should I pack? Like food?
Me: Diapers.
Tourist: Why?
Me: In case you actually saw a Giraffe or Penguin.
Tourist: This is ridiculous. You aren't really a tour guide or information center are you?!
Me: No, I'm not.
Tourist: Why did you say you were?
Me: I could tell that you were going to ask ridiculous questions, so I didn't want to miss it!
Tourist: That's not right!
Me: Ok. I apologize. I'll be serious. So, when are you going hiking in the Mountains?
Tourist: I'm not.
Me: Huh?
Tourist: I didn't bring any warmer clothes.
Me: Warmer clothes? It's got to be freezing up there! Like fifteen degrees!
Tourist: But you said it was warmer?!
Me: Did someone send you to me?
Tourist: No, why?
Me: Just curious.

#86 BUNGEE JUMPERS

Tourist: Hey, maybe you can help us?
Me: Maybe.
Tourist: We are wanting to go Bungee Jumping, but don't know where the best place is.
Me: Are you looking for a really high jump or a short one?
Tourist: High as possible.
Me: Cord or no cord?
Tourist: What? A cord of course!
Me: So, you want a boring jump, correct?
Tourist: Ummm, no! We want a HIGH jump!
Me: But with a cord.
Tourist: Yes, for safety.
Me: That's no fun.
Tourist: So you jump without a cord?
Me: Of course not. I won't jump at all. I'm afraid of heights.
Tourist: Figures.
Me: I'll jump off that park bench though if you want. Without a cord.
Tourist: No, that's Ok. We will just go ask someone else.
Me: Fine. I'm still going to jump off that park bench without a cord.
Tourist: You do that.
Me: I will.
Tourist: Ok.
Me: Will you do me a favor?
Tourist: Probably not, but ask.
Me: If something happens, go in the back and tell my wife.
Tourist: Seriously, what could happen?
Me: I might twist my ankle. I know it's risky, but I'm gonna do it.
Tourist: Have fun.
Me: If you're not going to stick around and tell my wife, I'm not going to do it. It's too risky.
Tourist: Are you Ok?
Me: Ummmm....

#87 THE TRIPPING WOMAN

Tourist: (After getting up from falling) Hey, did you see that?
Me: Yes! Are you Ok?
Tourist: I guess. What did I trip on?
Me: The sidewalk.
Tourist: I know that, but what made me trip?
Me: The sidewalk.
Tourist: Really?
Me: Yup.
Tourist: They should fix it!
Me: Well, you aren't the first one to trip.
Tourist: Have you told anybody to fix it?
Me: Nope.
Tourist: Why?
Me: Because I like watching people trip.
Tourist: That's not funny.
Me: No, not if you're tripping.
Tourist: You should tell someone.
Me: Who?
Tourist: The City.
Me: The City is not a person.
Tourist: You know what I mean.
Me: Ok. Fine. Should I tell them to remove the Pigeons too?
Tourist: Why?
Me: They make people trip all the time.
Tourist: Then yes.
Me: Ok. Baby strollers too?
Tourist: That's ridiculous.
Me: No, it's not. Crazy babies in strollers tripping people. It's a nuisance.
Tourist: You are being ridiculous.
Me: Well, I don't want to see innocent people tripping.... Wait, I take that back.

Short and Stupid

Tourist: Hey, are you from here?
Me: Yes.
Tourist: That's cool.
Me: Is that it?
Tourist: Yeah. I was just wondering.
Me: Ok. That was just awkward.
Tourist: Why?
Me: Because I lied. I'm not from here.
Tourist: Why did you say you were?
Me: Because I thought we were going to have a longer conversation and I wanted to act like I knew everything.
Tourist: Oh.

Excuse me Sir, we appear to be lost. Could you tell us…..hey look, Taffy!

~Why~

#81 NO

Tourist: Excuse me Sir, could you help me?
Me: No. It's Monday. Go away.

I had to end this with another Clown.

WEBSITE

WWW.COMEDIANALEXSTOKES.COM

FACEBOOK

MESSING WITH TOURISTS
ALEX STOKES
M.L.C. COMICS

TWITTER

COMEDIAN ALEX STOKES

GOOGLE +

COMEDIAN ALEX STOKES

GLOSSARY OF TERMS

OH JUST FORGET IT, I'M TIRED OF WRITING.

ABOUT THE AUTHOR

Alex Stokes is a Stand Up Comedian, Author, and Public Speaker from Sevierville, TN. He currently resides in the Gatlinburg area with his wife Jenny and their four boys. Growing up in one of the most popular tourist destinations in America, he became familiar with the ever changing landscape and pure craziness that a tourist area possesses. This history, combined with his most recent dealings with the public, led to the creation of this book.

Alex's Stand Up career began over three years ago after a fourteen year stint as an Investment Broker and Financial Planner. Within the first year, he had won several Stand Up Comedy contests and was awarded his first Feature spot opening for a Nationally touring comedian. Also, in that first year, Alex teamed up with fellow Comedians Sandy Goddard and Jay Pinkerton, forming the "M.L.C. Comics" and touring across the country to Los Angeles. Since that incredible first year, he has performed all around the country in comedy clubs, festivals, and charity events.

Alex is a true life storyteller when he's on stage as a Stand Up Comedian. His stories often times make fun of himself, embarking upon a crazy past that includes a short time playing college basketball, his career as an investment broker, and his family. However, most of these stories usually end with an unforeseen twist, leaving the audience to laugh hysterically while shaking their heads.

Alex earned his degree in Literature from the University of Tennessee, Knoxville, in 1997. This book, as Alex claims, is the first time he has used punctuation and grammar since his graduation. Even saying that he used it in this book, according to him, is a stretch. He is excited to share his stories and events in the book with anyone who is ready for a good laugh. It is his goal that each and every person who reads it finds the unorganized and unconventional style to be both refreshing and hilarious.

Made in the USA
Charleston, SC
01 November 2014